T0114780

Lessons
from the
Breakfast Table

Keys to Success from A to Z

Brian Blatt

BALBOA.PRESS
A DIVISION OF HAY HOUSE

Balboa Press books may be ordered through booksellers or by contacting:

Balboa Press
A Division of Hay House
1663 Liberty Drive
Bloomington, IN 47403
www.balboapress.com
844-682-1282

Print information available on the last page.

ISBN: 979-8-7652-2727-5 (sc)
ISBN: 979-8-7652-2729-9 (hc)
ISBN: 979-8-7652-2728-2 (e)

Library of Congress Control Number: 2022906623

Balboa Press rev. date: 05/23/2022

CONTENTS

CHAPTER 1

A is for ATTITUDE

Sophie and her brother Declan were very active kids. They played sports, took piano lessons, had many friends and did quite well in school.

One day Sophie, Declan and their parents volunteered with Sophie's soccer team. They put meals together for those in need. On the way home, Sophie asked, "Why do some people have big houses, fancy cars and swimming pools, while others barely have enough food to eat?"

Mom reflected, "There are some poor countries, and we should be very thankful to live in the country that we do." Sophie, being very astute replied, "So why are there poor people in our country?"

Dad explained, "There are many different reasons. Some people were never taught the keys to be successful. Some people knew some of the keys but chose to make poor decisions."

"Probably, some were not lucky!" chimed Declan.

Mom remarked, "That may be true Buddy, but regardless of how much or how little luck a person has, making good decisions will always lead you to success."

"Always?" Sophie questioned. "Always," her mom winked.

"So, what are the keys to success?" Sophie wanted to know.

Declan joked, "That's easy, it's the car keys!"

"Funny Buddy. No, we are not talking about car keys. There are several keys, and we've taught you many of them already," said Dad.

"Well how will we remember them?" wondered Declan.

"If you can remember the alphabet, you can remember these important keys!" exclaimed Mom.

Sophie giggled, "So what's the key that begins with the letter 'X'?"

"We'll get there, but how about we begin with the letter 'A'. Each week we'll focus on a different letter of the alphabet and see how we can apply that key," described Mom.

"Okay," said Sophie. "The letter 'A' is the beginning to which key?"

"'A' is for **ATTITUDE,**" Dad announced. "It's appropriate that this is the first word. Your attitude will determine your outcome more than anything else. This is an extremely important building block. If you have a poor, negative **ATTITUDE**, your results will be poor and negative. On the other hand, with a positive, can-do **ATTITUDE**, there are no limits to what you can achieve."

"That makes sense!" cheered Sophie. "During soccer events, I've been telling myself that I'm as good as any girl on the field and that confidence has helped me get better. I even scored two goals in my last game!"

"Exactly," Dad agreed.

"Let's see what other examples of good and bad **ATTITUDES** we can think of and see how they affected the outcome," stated Mom.

"What about the US women's soccer team?" asked Mom. "Do you think they had a positive or a negative **ATTITUDE** when they started out training for the 2019 World Cup?"

"A great **ATTITUDE**!" shouted Declan. "It's easy to have a great **ATTITUDE** when you've won the World Cup," he continued.

"Yes, but don't you think the team and coaches had a positive **ATTITUDE** from the beginning?" questioned Mom.

"Of course," Sophie added. "Does that mean that all the teams that didn't win had a bad **ATTITUDE?**" she questioned.

"No," Mom replied. "I'm sure most of the teams had a positive **ATTITUDE**. To represent their country, each person had to train for years to develop into the best Soccer player they could be. Trust me, you will not commit that much time and effort without a positive **ATTITUDE**."

"I see," Sophie nodded. "Are you born with either a good or bad **ATTITUDE?**

"I don't think so," answered Dad. "You must guard your **ATTITUDE**. It is very easy to be influenced by those around you. Many people look for all the reasons why something won't work. They often look for the downside. This is why so many bad things are shown in the news.

For some strange reason, people seem to prefer talking about the negative. If you continuously think and talk about why things are so difficult, you are developing a poor **ATTITUDE**."

"Got it!" exclaimed Declan. "So, if we keep a positive **ATTITUDE**, can we achieve anything we want?"

"Not necessarily," Mom responded. "However, it's one of the key principles and has a very big effect on what you ultimately accomplish. Think of **ATTITUDE** as the gasoline or electricity to your vehicle. Plenty of good **ATTITUDE** will give you the energy you need to continue on your path, especially when the road gets bumpy."

The next day at the dinner table, Sophie was excited to share how she used a good **ATTITUDE** at school.

"I thought about keeping a positive **ATTITUDE** all day," Sophie grinned. "I thanked my teachers, the lunch lady and my bus driver today. When I praised them each with a thank you, they returned big smiles. I could tell it made them happy."

"That's terrific!" praised Mom. "What about you Declan? Did you keep a positive **ATTITUDE** today?"

"Yep!" he boasted. "I helped my friend with numbers!"

"That's great!" Dad laughed. "So, does having a positive **ATTITUDE** help?"

"It helps," Sophie concluded. "However, sometimes it's hard to have a positive **ATTITUDE** when things aren't going well."

"Exactly and that's when it's especially important

to keep a good **ATTITUDE**," Dad pointed out. "Just understand that it is extremely important to have a good **ATTITUDE**. We'll uncover additional words that will help you keep a constant positive **ATTITUDE** as the weeks progress. In the meantime, keep focusing on that positive **ATTITUDE** this week. **BELIEVE** me that next week we'll uncover another important principle that will help to strengthen your **ATTITUDE**."

CHAPTER 2

B is for BELIEVE

After a week of positive **ATTITUDES** and words of encouragement, Sunday morning came. The kids were excited to find out what word would come this week. At the breakfast table, Mom announced, "This week is the letter 'B' and 'B' is for **BELIEFS**. As important as **ATTITUDE** is to determine the outcome, **BELIEFS** are equally, if not more important. You see, it is through **BELIEVING** that you gain the strength to keep a positive **ATTITUDE** especially when things go wrong."

"At your core, you must **BELIEVE** that you can accomplish anything you set your mind to. Your **BELIEF** sets everything else in motion. If you **BELIEVE** something is not possible, it surely will not be. However, should you dare to **BELIEVE** it is possible, well then, you have opened a door of possibility," explained Dad.

"I **BELIEVE** I can fly!" shouted Declan.

"Well, if you truly want to fly, you can get your pilot's license when you are older," replied Mom.

"I **BELIEVE** we're going to win our soccer tournament!" proclaimed Sophie.

"Me too!" agreed Dad.

Dad continued, "Let me tell you the story of Roger

Bannister. He was the first person to break the four-minute mile. Before then, practically everyone thought this was an impossible feat. They did not **BELIEVE** it could be done. Can you guess who **BELIEVED** it was possible?"

"Mr. Bannister?" Sophie inquired.

"That's right." Dad acknowledged. "On May 6, 1954, he broke the four-minute barrier. With that single race, Roger proved that it was possible!

The ancient games date back to 776 BC," Dad continued.

"That is 2,796 years ago," noted Sophie.

"Correct and until Roger ran the sub four-minute mile, people **BELIEVED** this was not possible. As a result, no human had ever achieved it. So, with little to no **BELIEF** from 776 BC to 1954…"

"Hold on Dad," interrupted Sophie. "How many years is that?"

"Do you **BELIEVE** if you take your time and work it out on paper, you can figure that out?" encouraged Mom.

"Yes!" exclaimed Sophie. After a minute, Sophie looked up and said, "2,730."

"Is she right?" Declan wondered.

"That's correct," replied Mom.

"In 2,730 years, not a single human had achieved this feat. Mr. Bannister certainly proved it was in fact possible for someone to break the four-minute mile. Do you know how many people have achieved that since then?"

"Twenty!" shouted Declan.

"More than that," replied Dad.

"Fifty?" guessed Sophie.

"Keep going!" encouraged Dad.

"One hundred?" asked Declan.

"Nope. Keep going!" Dad chanted.

"A Thousand?" Mom guessed.

"More!" cheered Dad.

"Just tell us!" pleaded Declan.

"Over 1,500 people!" Dad exclaimed.

Sophie questioned this, "You mean that in 2,730 years, not a single human ran a sub four-minute mile because people did not **BELIEVE** it was possible? In the next sixty-six years after that, people have understood and **BELIEVED** it to be possible? So therefore 1,500 people have now accomplished this goal?"

"Incredible, huh!" smiled Dad.

"That's amazing!" Sophie realized in astonishment.

"**BELIEVING** is very powerful," acknowledged Mom. "You kids are living at a time when there are more possibilities than ever before. It is up to each of you to **BELIEVE** in yourselves and make the correct **CHOICES** to achieve your **DREAMS**".

While winking at Mom, Dad said, "I wonder what word will be next week?"

Smiling back, Mom answered, "Great question. I hope we make a wise **CHOICE**."

Declan proclaimed, "Until then, I **BELIEVE** that those eggs are going to feel good in my belly!"

CHAPTER 3

C is for CHOICE

The following Sunday morning, as Sophie, Declan, Mom and Dad gathered for breakfast, Sophie announced, "I **BELIEVE** this week's word will provide another good lesson!"

"I **BELIEVE** you are correct," agreed Dad.

"What a great **ATTITUDE** you have," complimented Mom.

"I **BELIEVE** I know what the word will be this week," stated Declan.

"Let's hear it," Mom replied.

"Cookies!" shouted Declan.

"Interesting. Can you explain how cookies are relevant?" asked Dad.

"I don't know, but I sure do like them," Declan said with a smile.

"Okay," confirmed Sophie. "We're ready. What is the word this week?" she inquired.

"'C' is for **CHOICES**," instructed Mom. "Every **CHOICE** you make has a consequence."

"Every **CHOICE?**" questioned Sophie.

"Every **CHOICE**," Dad remarked.

Mom continued, "You see, no matter how big or how

small, every **CHOICE** you make results in a consequence. Sometimes the consequence is little, and sometimes it's big. Sometimes it's good and sometimes it's bad. Sometimes the **CHOICE** brings you closer to where you want to be and sometimes it takes you further away. Remember, every time your **CHOICE** ends in some type of result."

"Sounds like a lot to think about," murmured Sophie.

"It can be," said Dad. "However, when all else fails, simply **CHOOSE** to do the right thing. You'll know what the right thing is."

Mom inquired, "Can either of you give us some examples of **CHOICES** you've made".

"I **CHOSE** to stand up for a friend who was being bullied on the bus last week," Sophie shared.

"That's terrific! Now what was the consequence of that **CHOICE**?" asked Mom.

"The bully stopped, and it made my friend feel better," explained Sophie.

"How did that make you feel?" inquired Mom.

"I felt glad that I stood up for my friend," boasted Sophie.

"That makes us very proud," proclaimed Dad. "Now what about the **CHOICE** that the bully made?"

"That was a bad **CHOICE,**" Declan sighed.

"What were the consequences of that bad **CHOICE?**" asked Mom.

"He not only hurt my friend's feelings, but he also got

in trouble with the bus driver. Now he has to ride the bus in the front and sit by himself," Sophie explained.

"Declan, what about you? Can you give us an example of a **CHOICE** you made recently?" asked Dad?

"At school last week, I was working on my homework while other kids were goofing off," recalled Declan.

"What was the consequence of that **CHOICE?**" questioned Mom.

"My homework was finished before I got home and it gave me more time to play with my friends after school," Declan proudly admitted.

"Very good," asserted Mom. "What do you think the consequence was for the kids who were goofing off in the classroom?"

"Well, they either did not get their homework done or they had to do it when they were at home instead of playing with their friends," Declan guessed.

"That's right," reassured Dad. "You see, every **CHOICE** you make leads to a result. It's as simple as good **CHOICES** lead to good results and poor **CHOICES** lead to poor results.

"Now let me see if I'm getting this...

Keep a positive **ATTITUDE!**

BELIEFS lead to achievements!

Always make good **CHOICES!**" exclaimed Sophie.

"You bet!" Mom cheered. "If you continue to do these three things, you'll be able to achieve anything you want."

"Like what?" inquired Declan.

"Great question!" acknowledged Dad. "What do you want to achieve?"

"I want to win the Green Jacket!" Declan exclaimed.

"That sounds like a lofty **DREAM,**" his mom said with a smile.

"Yep, the Green Jacket!" Declan said with a sparkle in his eye.

"I want to play on the USA women's soccer team!" added Sophie.

"Another lofty **DREAM,**" noted Mom.

"Well let's focus this week on making excellent **CHOICES** and by the end of this week, you will both be a little wiser, healthier and a little closer to those **DREAMS,**" affirmed Dad.

"Now Sophie, make a wise **CHOICE** and pass your dad the bowl of fruit!"

CHAPTER 4

D is for DREAMS

The following Sunday morning, Sophie went to the chalk
board in the kitchen and wrote:

'A' is for Attitude!
'B' is for Beliefs!
'C' is for Choices!

She then looked at her mom and dad and asked, "What
does the letter 'D' stand for?"

Declan shouted, "'D' is for Declan!"

"No, 'D' is for Daddy," Sophie replied.

"How about diamonds?" wondered Mom as she smiled
at Dad.

"Okay," affirmed Dad. "Those are all great guesses! But
none are the next key. 'D' is for **DREAMS**"

"**DREAMS**?" inquired Sophie.

"**DREAMS,**" stated Dad.

"You mean like the **DREAMS** I have when I sleep?"
asked Declan.

"Sort of," spoke Mom. "However, the **DREAMS** you
have when you sleep, are less important than the **DREAMS**
you have when you are awake!"

"Awake? How do you **DREAM** when you are awake?" questioned Declan.

"Remember last week when we said if you continue to use the three keys..."

"**ATTITUDE, BELIEF** and **CHOICE!**" cried Sophie.

"Correct and remember we spoke about what you could achieve?" Mom continued.

"Oh yes, I remember," blurted Sophie. I said, "I want to be on the USA women's soccer team!"

"I want to win the Green Jacket!" cheered Declan.

"Well, those are examples of **DREAMS**," explained Dad. "Those **DREAMS** provide the spark to light a fire within you."

"A fire!" exclaimed Declan.

"A fire is an expression," replied Mom. "In this case, the expression is a strong desire for something that you really want."

"The exciting part is that there is no **DREAM** that you cannot achieve," proclaimed Dad.

"You mean we can achieve *ANY* **DREAM?**" wondered Sophie.

"Any **DREAM,**" answered Mom.

"Do you remember the story of Roger Bannister?" asked Dad.

"He was the first person to break the four-minute mile," Sophie pointed out. "He did that because he **BELIEVED** he could," she added.

"Very good," praised Dad. "He certainly did **BELIEVE**

he could do it. Before he **BELIEVED** he could do it, he had the **DREAM** to do it."

"So, he **DREAMED** it first, and then **BELIEVED**?" inquired Sophie.

"That's right," said Mom. "Because he **BELIEVED**, he kept a good **ATTITUDE** and made the **CHOICE** to train when no one else did," Mom added.

Declan sat there quietly.

"What are you thinking about?" questioned Mom.

"Well," he suspected. "What if there is more than one thing you **DREAM** about?"

"That's great," Mom insisted. "You can have more than one **DREAM**. In fact, you should have several **DREAMS**."

"You should?" Declan wondered.

"Of course," Dad acknowledged. "Think about my **DREAMS**. Your mother was my **DREAM** wife before we met. When I was younger, I had sports **DREAMS**, education **DREAMS** and money **DREAMS**. As a matter of fact, I have more **DREAMS** today than I did when I was your age."

"Wow!" realized Sophie. "I better start **DREAMING** more."

"You have plenty of time," assured Mom. "Remember, you're never too young to **DREAM** and you're never too old to **DREAM** either."

"This is going to be a fun week," Declan said, as he smiled.

"That's great," Mom agreed. "Also remember, there is a

time and place for everything. When you're at school, you need to focus on your **EDUCATION**"

"Ugh," grumbled Declan. "I know, I know".

"DREAM on your own time kids," Dad instructed. "Listen to your teachers. They're working hard to provide you both with a solid **EDUCATION**. In the meantime, my **DREAM** is a cup of coffee!"

"Funny Dad," Sophie giggled, as she went to the chalkboard and added: D is for **DREAM**.

CHAPTER 5

E is for EDUCATION

The following Sunday, Declan grabbed the chalk and asked his parents what the letter 'E' was going to stand for.

"Your father and I have been giving you the 'E' word since we've begun these Sunday morning lessons," said Mom.

"Eggs?" asked Declan.

"Haha," laughed Sophie. "Okay, Attitude, Believe, Choice, Dream... hmmmm." What do these words have in common?" thought Sophie.

"Think about it," requested Dad. "What have we been giving you each time we taught you the importance of a word?"

"Keys!" shouted Declan.

"Yes Buddy, we certainly have been *TEACHING* important keys," asserted Mom. "What else have we been giving you with these valuable lessons?" she inquired.

"An **EDUCATION**!" exclaimed Sophie.

"That's right!" agreed Mom.

"I thought you have to go to school to get an **EDUCATION**," stated Declan.

"That's correct that you go to school to get an **EDUCATION**," responded Dad. "However, those who constantly strive for their **DREAMS**, never stop pursuing their **EDUCATION**. If you want to become very successful, you must treat school as only the beginning to your **EDUCATION**."

"Only the beginning?" questioned Sophie. "What about when we graduate from high school?" she asked.

"You'll move on to the next part of your **EDUCATION**, which will likely be college," assured Mom.

"What about when we graduate from college?" Sophie questioned.

"You'll continue your **EDUCATION** by learning skills needed at work," confirmed Dad.

"What if I decide to start my own company?" Sophie challenged.

"Then you better accelerate your **EDUCATION**," proclaimed Mom.

"What school is after college?" Sophie questioned.

"There are many other types of formal **EDUCATION**. These include receiving your Masters, Doctorate, Law degree and hundreds of other types of licenses and certificates," Mom specified.

"Wow, that's a lot of **EDUCATION!**" cried Declan.

"Okay," said Sophie. "Then we're done, right?" she questioned.

"Only if you **CHOOSE** to be done," declared Dad. "If you have a **DREAM** and are determined to **BELIEVE** in yourself, maintain a positive **ATTITUDE**, then you will pursue your **DREAM** by taking constant action. As you learn from the positive and negative outcomes along the way, you are **EDUCATING** yourself throughout the process," Dad continued.

"That's right," said Mom. "You can and must learn from your **mistakes**, but what if we told you, it's likely that someone else has done what you're trying to achieve. What if I told you that it's likely that there are books, podcasts and YouTube clips providing the many lessons learned along their journey. Wouldn't it make sense for you to seek out those lessons and learn from them rather than through your own **mistakes**?"

"I see," replied Sophie. "So, by us reading and learning, whether it's in school or on our own, we are receiving an **EDUCATION**."

"Exactly," smiled Dad. "Those who constantly seek **EDUCATION** will separate themselves from the pack."

"Think of **EDUCATION** as giving you the map to where you are trying to go," added Mom. "Sure, you can drive across the country to a **DREAM** destination using your wit and determination, but don't you think it would be helpful to have a map?"

"Yea, that wouldn't be much fun to drive by yourself without a map," Declan admitted.

"It also wouldn't be fun if you had to carry with you other people's luggage. Would it?" questioned Dad.

"Why would you ever go on a road trip with someone else's luggage?" wondered Sophie. "I would barely have room for my own bags!"

"That's right," agreed Dad. "You'd be surprised how easy it is to carry other people's bags and how often people do this."

"What are you talking about?" asked Declan.

"You must **FORGIVE** me," Dad answered. "We'll get into that lesson next week."

"Now let me **EDUCATE** you on how I am feeling," grumbled Dad. "I'm hungry!"

CHAPTER 6

F is for FORGIVENESS

The following Sunday, Sophie and Declan gathered for breakfast. Sophie asked, "What **EDUCATION** will we be receiving today?"

"I got the chalk!" shouted Declan.

"This week's lesson, while simple, can often be one of the toughest ones to apply consistently," said Mom.

"If it's simple, why would it be tough to apply?" wondered Sophie.

"When you don't need it, you understand the importance of it," Dad added. "When it's time to use this word, you are often filled with negative emotions that cloud your mind making it difficult to use."

"When we don't need it, we understand the importance. However, when we do need it, we often are blinded by our emotions?" Sophie asked.

"This seems like a tricky one," cried Declan. "So, what's the word?"

"**FORGIVENESS**," stated Mom.

"**FORGIVENESS**?" questioned Sophie.

"That's right," confirmed Dad.

"I know it's important to **FORGIVE** others. What does

that have to do with achieving our **DREAMS**?" Sophie wondered.

"Do you remember when we ended last week's discussion about **EDUCATION** being the road map that helps show you how to get to your destination?" Dad asked.

"Yes, I remember," said Declan.

"Yes, and you said something about carrying other people's luggage," recalled Sophie.

"Exactly," Dad affirmed. "You see, as you grow up, there will be many times when someone does something wrong to you. It may be something they said, something they did or something they didn't do. The point is, throughout life your ego will be bruised from time to time and someone will surely cause the pain."

"That's not nice!" exclaimed Declan.

"No, it's not," Mom agreed. "Your Dad is right. Life will not always be fair."

"If someone does something to hurt you or your brother or sister, it's okay to stand up for yourselves. We're not saying to let a bully continue to harm you. After you let the other person know that you will not stand for that behavior, you must learn to **FORGIVE** and let go of angry feelings."

"That's hard to do," admitted Sophie.

"We know it is," said Dad. "This is why we said this word is simple, but tough."

"You kids understand that **FORGIVING** others is part

of being good children and doing what God has taught us to do, right?" Dad asked.

"We know," assured Declan.

"By **FORGIVING** others, you are releasing their burden that is holding you down. It's like taking that road trip and always being weighed down with other people's baggage. The more you hold on to the grudge and resentment in your heart, the heavier their baggage is that you are carrying around. You need forgiveness because it will free you."

"That wouldn't be a fun way to travel to your destination," remarked Declan.

"Another way to think about it is not **FORGIVING**. This is like drinking a witch's potion in hopes that it will hurt the other person," warned Mom.

"That's crazy!" exclaimed Sophie. "Why would anyone drink a witch's potion and expect it to hurt someone else?"

"Well, that's the same thing as holding onto negative thoughts about another person and expecting it to hurt the other person," Mom explained. "The only person that it is hurting is yourself."

"That's right," said Dad. "Remember how important our first lesson was with a positive **ATTITUDE**?"

"Sure do," said Declan.

"It's impossible to have a positive **ATTITUDE** and hold a grudge against another person at the same time. It won't be easy, but you must always **FORGIVE**," emphasized Mom.

"I **FORGIVE** you Sophie for taking the last piece of toast," acknowledged Declan.

"Thank you, Declan," Sophie responded.

"Do you see how **FORGIVING** someone immediately unlocks **GRATITUDE**," said Mom as she smiled at Dad.

"What-itude?" inquired Declan.

"I beg your **FORGIVENESS**, but we'll cover 'what-itude' next week," laughed Dad.

CHAPTER 7

G is for GRATITUDE

The following Sunday came as quickly as they all do. This Sunday was extra special because it was Declan's birthday! After early church, Sophie, Declan, Mom and Dad went out for brunch. They went to their favorite place, Standard Service. The food there is always terrific, and they have many games for the children outside. It was a real treat!

Normally, the kids would be off playing just as soon as the car was put into park. However, this time it was different, for it was Sunday morning and time for another lesson around the table.

"Mom, what's today's word?" asked Sophie.

"That's a good question," Mom replied. "What word did we discuss last week?"

"**FOREGIVENESS**," Sophie responded.

"Yeah," added Declan. "We did **ATTITUDE**, **BELIEFS**, **CHOICES**, **DREAMS**... my favorite, **EDUCATION** and **FORGIVENESS**. Now we're on the letter 'G.'"

"You've been paying attention," said Dad. "That makes your mother and me very happy. We're very **GRATEFUL** that you're paying attention."

"Of course!" cried Declan. "This is fun."

"Today's word is **GRATITUDE**," spoke Mom.

"Oh yeah, the What-itude word," remembered Declan.

"**GRATITUDE** means the same thing as **GRATEFUL**," explained Sophie. "It means to be **THANKFUL**."

"Why didn't we just say **THANKFUL?**" questioned Declan.

"Easy, because **THANKFUL** does not begin with the letter 'G'," stated Sophie.

"Right again there, Missy," acknowledged Dad.

"Is this why you always remind us to say thank you?" asked Declan.

"Exactly," agreed Mom. "Expressing **GRATITUDE**, by saying **THANK YOU**, can make such an impact on the other person. Saying those two words costs you nothing and it shows the other person that you really appreciate what he or she has done for you. It lets you show them that you don't take them for granted."

At that time, the waitress brought the drinks. Without being reminded by Mom or Dad, both kids said "**THANK YOU**" with a big smile. The waitress smiled from ear to ear replying, "You bet kids!"

"That made her happy," noticed Declan. "She had a big smile."

"How did that make you feel?" inquired Mom.

"Great!" exclaimed Sophie.

"Now kids, let me tell you the story of when I really learned the importance of **GRATITUDE**," Dad said.

"When I was sixteen, my brother and I stayed the summer with our Uncle Albert."

"Is that when you got your pilot's license?" questioned Sophie.

"Correct," affirmed Dad. "Well after one of my flight lessons with Uncle Albert, he said to me, "Brian, how many times have we flown?""

"I don't know," I replied. "Maybe five or six times."

Uncle Albert answered, "That sounds about right. Do you realize that not one time have you said **THANK YOU**?"

"What a punch in the gut. Your Daddy felt about one inch tall."

"Dad, you always say **THANK YOU**," insisted Sophie.

"That is the biggest reason why," admitted Dad.

"With that one sentence, I realized that I was taking him for granted. I vowed to myself from that day forward, no one would ever think of me as being inconsiderate. I never let an opportunity pass me by without showing the other person my **GRATITUDE**," Dad remarked.

"Dad, is that why you always make us wave when we walk in front of a vehicle at the store?" wondered Declan.

"Precisely," specified Dad. "Even though you're in a cross-walk and have the right of way, it just shows a sign of appreciation to the driver."

At that time, the waitress returned to take everyone's order.

"I'm trying to decide between the veggie omelet or the salmon bagel," mumbled Mom.

"They are both great, but my favorite is the salmon bagel," suggested the waitress.

"**THANK YOU**, that was very **HELPFUL.** I'll have your favorite," decided Mom.

They had a great brunch, after which was celebrated with a birthday song and cupcakes.

"Declan, I'm sure **GRATEFUL** that it's your birthday!" cheered Sophie.

CHAPTER 8

H is for HELPFUL

Sunday morning came and before Mom and Dad could finish their first cup of coffee, Sophie and Declan came running down the stairs.

Sophie went to the chalk board and read:

"Have a positive **ATTITUDE!**
BELIEFS lead to achievements!
Make good **CHOICES!**
Chase your **DREAMS!**
EDUCATION does not end at school!
FORGIVENESS to all others!
Always give **GRATITUDE!**"

"Today is 'H'," said Declan.

"Any guesses?" questioned Dad.

"Hello?" inquired Sophie.

"Saying hello to someone is good," stated Mom. "What else begins with the letter 'H' and is more **HELPFUL?**"

"Hmmm…," hummed Declan.

"Would a hint be **HELPFUL?**" asked Mom as she smiled at Dad.

"**HELP!**" shouted Sophie.

"Very good," affirmed Dad. "Not only is **HELPING** others the right thing to do, but it is also a great way to attract **HELP** from others."

"Now remember the intent of your **HELP** can be just as important as the **HELP** itself. If you only **HELP** someone else because you expect something in return, most likely you will be disappointed and left holding a grudge against that person," Mom explained.

"I don't want to hold other people's bags," replied Declan.

"Exactly," acknowledged Dad. "When you freely **HELP** others and expect nothing in return, that is when the magic happens."

"Magic?" wondered Sophie.

"Magic," agreed Mom. "Imagine that every thought and every action you have is sent out into the universe and will return to you sometime in the future magnified. It works both ways. So, if you say something bad about another person, more people will speak bad about you in the future. However, if you have good intentions and **HELP** others, **HELP** will return to you at a time when you need it."

"That's like what that guy said with funny hair," remarked Sophie.

"Einstein?" questioned Dad.

"Yeah," asserted Sophie. "Didn't he say that for every action, there is an equal and opposite reaction?"

"Wow, very impressive. However, it was Sir Isaac Newton

that discovered that universal law," noted Dad. "This law refers to matter and energy, but many believe this is also true with thoughts and actions and is referred to as karma."

"Now regardless of whether you believe in this magic or not, being **HELPFUL** to others without expecting anything in return, is always the right thing to do. You can never go wrong by doing something that is right," emphasized Mom.

"Yep, there's never a wrong time to do the right thing," added Dad.

"Plus, being **HELPFUL** makes you feel good inside," Sophie shouted.

"It sure does," answered Mom. "Let's see how much you kids can **HELP** out this week."

"Challenge accepted!" shouted Declan.

"And **HELPING** others will have both of you on the path to living with high **INTEGRITY**," said Dad while smiling at Mom.

"High **INTEGRITY**?" asked Declan.

"We'll get there, but first can you be a **HELPFUL** lad and pass me the milk," laughed Dad.

CHAPTER 9

I is for INTEGRITY

Another Sunday came and like the many Sundays before, Mom and Dad were enjoying their first cup of coffee when Sophie and Declan came down the stairs.

Declan shouted, "It's my turn to read the chalkboard!

> Have a positive **ATTITUDE!**
> **BELIEFS** lead to achievements!
> Make good **CHOICES!**
> Chase your **DREAMS!**
> **EDUCATION** does not end at school!
> **FORGIVENESS** to all others!
> Always give **GRATITUDE!**
> Give **HELP** to those in need!"

"What's the word today?" questioned Sophie.

"The letter 'I' stands for another very important word," said Mom. "'I' is for **INTEGRITY**."

"**INTEGRITY** means to do the right thing," replied Sophie.

"It's that simple," stated Dad. "Without **INTEGRITY**, nothing else matters."

"Why would nothing else matter?" inquired Declan.

"Because, if you lack **INTEGRITY** and are willing to cut corners, deceive others and put your personal gains above others. What you do achieve, will be built on a weak foundation," explained Mom.

"What do you mean?" inquired Declan.

"Well think of each achievement representing a floor on a skyscraper. The foundation is the base of the skyscraper and must be strong enough to support the entire weight of the skyscraper," described Dad.

"You better have a strong foundation!" exclaimed Sophie.

"That's right," agreed Mom. "You would want to make sure that foundation is firmly planted on strong soil and made with lots of concrete and rebar."

"What's rebar?" asked Declan.

"Rebar is metal rods placed in the concrete to help give it extra strength," defined Dad.

"The taller the skyscraper, the stronger and deeper the foundation better be," declared Mom. "The foundation must support the skyscraper for hundreds of years. Think of all of the rain and wind the skyscraper will see over its lifetime."

"Now what would happen if you tried to build a house, yet alone a skyscraper with the foundation made of straw on top of quicksand?" questioned Dad.

"The house would fall right down," grumbled Sophie.

"That's right," said Dad. "Why is that?" Dad asked.

"Because the foundation is weak," remarked Sophie.

"Right again," Dad declared.

"This seems really important. All we have to do is do the right thing?" asked Declan.

"It's really that simple," admitted Mom. "You see, having high **INTEGRITY** means you do the following:

Take responsibility for your actions.

Put others needs above your own.

Choose honesty in all matters.

Show respect to everyone.

Keep your promises."

"A person of high **INTEGRITY** can be trusted with big matters, because they have delivered on all the small matters," Dad confirmed. "You see, you can't say that you will handle the big matters with high **INTEGRITY** and fib with the smaller matters. Building **INTEGRITY** is like building a muscle and needs worked every day. The more you train your **INTEGRITY** muscle, the easier it will become to always make the right decision. Even when that decision puts you at a disadvantage."

"How do we know our **INTEGRITY** muscle is getting strong?" Declan wondered.

"When you find yourself always doing the right thing, especially when no one else is looking," Mom pointed out. "Remember, that foundation needs to hold the weight of the skyscraper even when everyone is asleep."

"Think of the **JOY** it will bring you when you know you're building your **INTEGRITY** muscle knowing that it will be strong enough to support the weight of a skyscraper," smiled Dad.

"Dad, I want to build a skyscraper as high as the Empire State Building," cheered Sophie.

"You can do it Sophie," encouraged Dad. "If you and Declan take to heart the lessons your Mom and I have been teaching and apply each one... someday, your achievements will make the Empire State Building look like a tree house!"

CHAPTER 10

J is for JOY

Sunday morning came once again, but this time Sophie was the first one downstairs. As Mom and Dad came down the steps, they saw Sophie staring at the chalkboard with the chalk in her hand.

> Have a positive **ATTITUDE!**
> **BELIEFS** lead to achievements!
> Make good **CHOICES!**
> Chase your **DREAMS!**
> **EDUCATION** does not end at school!
> **FORGIVENESS** to all others!
> Always give **GRATITUDE!**
> Give **HELP** to those in need!
> **INTEGRITY** is doing the right thing, even
> when no one is looking!
> 'J!'...

Sophie wondered, "What does the letter 'J' stand for?"

Mom smiled at Sophie and replied, "You'll like this word, but let's wait for your brother."

"Declan!" yelled Sophie. "Time to wake up!"

"Sophie, can you let your mom and I at least pour our first cup of coffee?" Dad asked.

"Awe, but Dad, I've been up for two hours," Sophie yawned.

"Two hours?" questioned Mom. "I guess you won't have a hard time going to sleep tonight."

At that time, Declan came stumbling down the stairs.

"Great, Declan is here!" exclaimed Sophie. "So, what does the letter 'J' stand for?"

"**JOY,**" stated Mom. "'J' stands for **JOY.**"

"I like **JOY,**" smiled Declan.

"So do I," spoke Sophie. "What does **JOY** have to do with helping us achieve our **DREAMS**?" wondered Sophie.

"Great question," confirmed Dad. "Let's look at the chalkboard and see how **JOY** fits in."

"'A' is for **ATTITUDE,**" read Declan.

"If you carry yourself in a **JOYFUL** manner, do you think it's easier or harder to maintain a positive **ATTITUDE**?" asked Dad.

"Easier," answered Sophie.

"Absolutely," affirmed Dad.

"What about the next word," questioned Mom.

"**BELIEFS** lead to achievements," read Sophie.

"If you keep **JOYFUL**, is it easier or harder to **BELIEVE** in yourself?" asked Mom.

"Definitely easier," Declan commented.

"That's right," assured Dad.

"Yeah, but the next one can be tricky," Sophie

admitted. "Sometimes it's easier to make poor **CHOICES** even though you know it's better for you to make the right **CHOICES**."

"Indeed," agreed Dad. "You will certainly be challenged with temptations. However, deep down you will always know what the right **CHOICE** is. For instance, you may be tempted to continue playing on your computer or watching TV when you know the right **CHOICE** is different. The better choice would be to finish your homework or complete your chores. While in the moment, you might think that you would experience more **JOY** making the wrong **CHOICE,** but that is not true. As you build your willpower, in the long run you will experience far deeper **JOY** by making the right **CHOICES**."

"The longer you've journeyed, the far more **JOYFUL** you will be when you finally achieve your **DREAMS**," said Mom. "It's like your dad's saying, 'The higher the climb, the better the view'."

"Precisely," acknowledged Dad. The more you've overcome **OBSTACLES** and **PERSERVERED**, the more gratification and **JOY** you will experience. If you combine that with the other keys that we've been discussing, you'll start to create an internal **JOY** that cannot be quenched."

"So, you're saying, the more disciplined we are at exercising the other keys, the more **JOYFUL** we will become. In keeping a **JOYFUL** heart, it will also help us continue to implement the other keys?" smiled Sophie.

"That's right," concluded Mom. "All of these lessons are interconnected. Think of them as 'The Circle of Life.'"

"Like the Lion King?" asked Declan.

"That's right Buddy," agreed Dad. "Think of these keys as Mufasa's secrets to running a kingdom."

"I'm Simba!" cheered Declan.

"Okay my little lion," grinned Mom. "Do you want to grow up to be a cruel king like Scar, or do you want to be a **KIND** King, like Mufasa?"

"I want to be **KIND** like Dad!" Declan shouted.

"Awe, thanks Buddy," winked Dad. "You have just given me the gift of **JOY** that will last a lifetime. Now, who is ready for pancakes?"

CHAPTER 11

K is for KINDNESS

The following Sunday, the kids came running down the steps.

"What time is it?" asked Dad.

"7:15," replied Mom.

"These kids are waking up earlier and earlier on Sunday mornings," said Dad as he took a sip of his coffee.

"What word is today," inquired Sophie.

"Yeah, what word," repeated Declan.

"Go through the list so we know what letter we're on," directed Mom.

> "Have a positive **ATTITUDE!**
> **BELIEFS** lead to achievements!
> Make good **CHOICES!**
> Chase your **DREAMS!**
> **EDUCATION** does not end at school!
> **FORGIVENESS** to all others!
> Always give **GRATITUDE!**
> Give **HELP** to those in need!
> **INTEGRITY** is doing the right thing, even
> when no one is looking!
> Smile with **JOY!**
> '**K!**'...

We're on the letter 'K,'" noted Sophie.

"The letter 'K' is for **KINDNESS,**" stated Mom.

"I knew it!" shouted Declan. "I was going to say that."

"Yeah, I thought so too," added Sophie.

"We told you these were simple lessons," admitted Dad. "However, don't mistake them being simple as not being important."

"Okay, so what does being **KIND** have to do with achieving your **DREAMS?**" questioned Sophie. "I know it's important to be **KIND** because I want to be a good person, but how does this help me become successful?"

"Let's look back at some of the important lessons we've already discussed," said Mom. "**FORGIVENESS, GRATITUDE, HELP, INTEGRITY** and **JOY**... In doing each one of these, you are being **KIND.**"

"Exactly," remarked Dad. "Remember how we said last week that the words are all interconnected like the circle of life."

"I remember Dad. I'm Simba," Declan roared.

"That's right little lion," acknowledged Dad. "Think of **KIND** as a power word that encompasses several of the other words together."

"That's right," agreed Mom. "If you accomplished your **DREAMS,** but you were not **KIND** to others along the way, how many friends do you think you'd have to celebrate with?"

"Not many," sighed Sophie.

"If any at all," agreed Mom.

"That doesn't sound very fun," murmured Declan.

"Now back to your earlier question Sophie. How does being **KIND** help you achieve your **DREAMS**?" asked Dad. "Imagine chasing your **DREAMS** as being the world's largest **OBSTACLE** course that's also a maze."

"Now that sounds fun!" cheered Declan.

"It can be, with the right **ATTITUDE**!" proclaimed Mom. "You must **BELIEVE** you would safely make it out of the maze a better person than when you began… Then that would be fun!"

"The reality is each **DREAM** comes with it. Each dream has its very own **OBSTACLE** maze course," declared Dad. "Some are bigger than others. Some have more **OBSTACLES.** Some have more dead ends. However, they all have people along the way that can help. If you are **KIND** to everyone on your adventure, do you think they will be more willing to help you when you need it?"

"Absolutely!" cried Sophie. "If I'm **KIND** and **HELP** others when they need it, they'll be more willing to be **KIND** and **HELP** me."

"I hope my **OBSTACLE** maze course has rope swings and climbing walls!" shouted Declan.

"Well, if your **DREAM** is to be an American Ninja Warrior, it will," affirmed Mom.

"I **LOVE** thinking that I'm in the world's biggest **OBSTACLE** maze course. When things get difficult, I'll just tell myself that it's just another **OBSTACLE** that I must overcome to get through the maze!" announced Sophie.

Declan walked over to Sophie and gave her a big hug and said, "I **LOVE** you Sis."

"Awe, that was so sweet Buddy," grinned Mom.

"I better be nice to Sophie. I'll probably need her help at some point in my **OBSTACLE** maze course," he recognized.

"Okay," confirmed Dad. "You just inspired me to be **KIND** and take us out to eat for breakfast!"

CHAPTER 12

L is for LOVE

Sunday morning came again, but this time both Sophie and Declan were up before Mom and Dad. As they were downstairs pouring their parents a cup of coffee Mom and Dad came walking down the steps.

"Awe, that is so sweet of you kids," said Mom.

"We wanted to do something **KIND** for you two and show you our **GRATITUDE** for being our Mom and Dad," said Sophie.

"We're proud of you two. We **LOVE** you so much," said Dad. "Okay Declan... to the board"

"Have a positive **ATTITUDE!**
BELIEFS lead to achievements!
Make good **CHOICES!**
Chase your **DREAMS!**
EDUCATION does not end at school!
FORGIVENESS to all others!
Always give **GRATITUDE!**
Give **HELP** to all others!
INTEGRITY is doing the right thing, even when no one is looking!
Smile with **JOY!**

Always show **KINDNESS**!

'**L**!'…

I think 'L' is for **LOVE**," said Declan.

"Excellent!" said Mom. "That's right. Your Dad and I **LOVE** you kids so much."

"We **LOVE** you guys too," replied Sophie.

"And Sophie **LOVE'S** her boyfriend," laughed Declan.

"Hey!" exclaimed Sophie. "I do not!"

"Okay," said Mom. "You two stop arguing."

"Mom, I think I can see why **LOVE** is important," said Sophie. "When you **LOVE** someone or even something, you will do and be all of the words that we have written on the chalk board."

"Very good Sophie," replied Dad. "The student is starting to become the teacher."

"But **LOVE** is tricky," Sophie said. "What about when someone makes me mad or it's someone I don't know?"

"**LOVE** is much more than a feeling," answered Dad. "While yes, **LOVE** is a powerful emotion that can inspire us to achieve great things, it is also a commitment that is rooted in faith."

"Why do these words always mean more than we first thought," said Declan.

"Because these words are key words," said Mom. "Now let's test what your dad said about **LOVE** being more than an emotion."

"Sophie," Mom continued, "Does your brother ever make you mad?"

"Yes," said Sophie as she smiled.

"Hey!" said Declan.

"Declan, does your sister ever make you mad?" asked Mom.

"Yep!" Declan quickly replied.

"Now what if there was a bully at school picking on your brother or sister," asked Mom.

"I would tell them to pick on someone their own size," said Sophie.

"I bet you would do it, regardless of whether you were mad at your brother or not," said Dad. "No matter what, the **LOVE** you have for your family will always be there whether you know it or not."

"What about **LOVE** for people who are not our family?" asked Sophie. "I know it's important to **LOVE** others, but that seems hard."

"You're right," said Mom. "But when you show **KINDNESS**, **GRATITUDE**, **FORGIVENESS** and **HELP** those in need, those are all actions that come from a place of **LOVE**. Think of **LOVE** as the sun while the light, heat and orbit of the Earth are all things that happen because of the sun. In a similar manner, **LOVE** creates these other acts."

"Your **LOVE** will help you have a good **ATTITUDE**, **BELIEVE** and make good **CHOICES**," added Declan.

"I think the kids have really been listening," Dad said with a big smile.

"I picture when we're going through our large **OBSTACLE** maze course, the **LOVE** we have within will act as a light and light up the dark corners of the maze."

"Wow!" said Mom. "That is an awesome way to look at it. Remember, all the **DREAMS** we chase require us going through a large maze with many **OBSTACLES** and dark corners. Your light will certainly come in handy."

"Yep," added Declan. "With good light, you won't make as many wrong turns."

"You mean like a **MISTAKE?**" Dad asked.

"Yes," said Declan. "When you see the dead-ends because of your light, you won't go down that direction."

"Interesting," said Dad. "I'd **LOVE** to hear more about this, but I would also **LOVE** to eat breakfast first."

CHAPTER 13

M is for MISTAKES

Once again it was Sunday morning. Mom and Dad came down the stairs to two kids pouring them coffee.

"Good morning," greeted Declan.

"Happy morning to you too," responded Mom.

"I'm **LOVING** the service from our waitress and waiter," smiled Dad.

"Look Mom, we even added whip cream to the coffee," boasted Sophie.

"I can get used to this," winked Mom.

"Okay Sophie," Dad said. "To the board."

"Have a positive **ATTITUDE!**
BELIEFS lead to achievements!
Make good **CHOICES!**
Chase your **DREAMS!**
EDUCATION does not end at school!
FORGIVENESSS to all others!
Always give **GRATITUDE!**
Give **HELP** to those in need!
INTEGRITY is doing the right thing, even when no one is looking!
Smile with **JOY!**

Always show **KINDNESS!**
LOVE always!
'M!'…

Is 'M' for money?" asked Sophie.

"Money is very important. By living a life that's filled with these words, money will not be in short supply," stated Dad. "Guess again."

"'M' is for muscle," guessed Declan.

"Yes, your physical health is very important, but muscle is not our key word for the letter 'M,'" said Mom.

"Music?" questioned Sophie.

"Another great word, but not today's word," relayed Dad.

"Okay, just tell us," begged Declan.

"'M' is for **MISTAKE,**" noted Mom.

"**MISTAKE!?!**" exclaimed Sophie with a puzzled look. "Why would a **MISTAKE** be important to help us achieve our **DREAMS?**"

"Do you remember how we ended last week's discussion on **LOVE?**" asked Mom.

"Yeah," recalled Sophie. "We said that **LOVE** is to **KINDNESS** and **GRATITUDE** like the sun is to light and heat. **LOVE** is the source that produces **KINDNESS** and **GRATITUDE.**"

"**LOVE** also helps with a good **ATTITUDE,** **BELIEVING** and making good **CHOICES,**" announced Declan.

"Correct," declared Mom. "Do you remember how we

also described **LOVE** as a light shining from within? Do you remember how helpful we said this **LOVE** would be in the **OBSTACLE** maze course?"

"Oh yeah," remembered Sophie.

"Yeah," Declan chimed in. "The light will help us see the dark paths that are dead-ends."

"Exactly," approved Dad. "What if the only way you could find out for sure is to try a path."

"That's easy," answered Declan. "You just move down that path until you learn that the path doesn't lead you where you are trying to go. Then, you simply just turn around and move towards the next path."

"So, while you're trying your best working towards your **DREAM**, there may be times you fall down or make a wrong decision, sort of like a **MISTAKE**?" inquired Mom.

"Well, yeah. I suppose so," shrugged Sophie.

"If in your **OBSTACLE** maze course, you make a **MISTAKE** should you be upset and give up? Or, should you mark your **MISTAKE** as a lesson learned and adjust accordingly?" questioned Dad.

"You may get upset or annoyed by your **MISTAKE**, but now you have new information that you didn't have before you made the **MISTAKE**," said Sophie.

"Precisely!" exclaimed Mom. "Would you two agree that the only way you will ever reach your **DREAM** at the end of your **OBSTACLE** maze course is by making hundreds or maybe even thousands of **MISTAKES**?"

"I wish we had a map of our **OBSTACLE** maze course," murmured Declan.

"What if you knew there were people who already completed the **OBSTACLE** maze course? Would it make sense to ask them for help?" asked Dad.

"Wouldn't that be cheating?" questioned Sophie.

"Nope. That's the amazing part," asserted Mom. "In this game of life, there have been many generations who lived before us. Depending on your **DREAM**, there are likely several people who have completed that **OBSTACLE** maze course. I'm sure they would love to **HELP**. All you have to do is ask for **HELP**."

"Don't take our word for it. I suggest you listen to what Jesus said: "Ask and it shall be given. Seek and you will find. Knock and it shall be opened to you," added Dad. "The only thing smarter than learning by your **MISTAKES** is learning through other people's **MISTAKES**."

"So, if someone had already gone down a path, we should ask them where it leads and whether it is a dead-end?" questioned Declan.

"Bingo," nodded Dad. "Asking others for **HELP** along the **OBSTACLE** maze course will save you a lot of time and frustration."

"Always remember, you must never become scared of making a **MISTAKE**," added Mom. "Sometimes, you will be in a place of the **OBSTACLE** maze course where you must simply decide and move. Sitting still will not get you any closer. If you make a **MISTAKE**, you now know more than you did before you made the **MISTAKE.** Therefore, you are that much closer in completing the **OBSTACLE** maze course and achieving your **DREAM**."

"Well, what if the maze leads us to the wilderness and it becomes dark and cold?" asked Sophie.

"That's when you must become **VALIENT,**" urged Dad.

"Say what?" inquired Declan.

"That means to be courageous," remarked Dad. "Don't worry, we'll get there. Sophie, if you find yourself alone in the wilderness, not only must you choose to be **VALIENT**, but you should simply observe what **NATURE** is doing."

"What does that mean?" Sophie questioned.

"That's enough for one morning," replied Mom. We'll get there next week. Remember this week is about recognizing that **MISTAKES** are a part of the **OBSTACLE** maze and are necessary in order for you to complete the maze to reach your **DREAM**."

CHAPTER 14

N is for NATURE

The following Sunday, as Mom and Dad came down the steps, not only did they find two cups of coffee at the table, but they each had a piece of toast on their plates.

"Wow," grinned Mom. "I'm really enjoying our Sunday mornings, but what is burning?"

"Well, we burnt a couple of pieces of toast before we figured out how to get it just right," admitted Declan.

"Yeah," agreed Sophie. "We learned from our **MISTAKE** and tried again. The second time we knew to turn down the heat setting on the toaster."

"Awesome!" exclaimed Dad. "See no reason to get angry. Just tell yourself, that was a **MISTAKE** and think what you need to do different next time. Great job!"

"Okay Declan, to the chalk board," ordered Mom.

"Have a positive **ATTITUDE!**
BELIEFS lead to achievements!
Make good **CHOICES!**
Chase your **DREAMS!**
EDUCATION does not end at school!
FORGIVENESS to all others!
Always give **GRATITUDE!**

Give **HELP** to those in need!
INTEGRITY is doing the right thing, even when no one is looking!
Smile with **JOY!**
Always show **KINDNESS!**
LOVE always!
MISTAKES are hidden lessons!
'N!'..."

"I remember," recalled Sophie. "'N' is for **NATURE**. This will be interesting."

"That's right," replied Mom. "You'll be amazed how many lessons we can learn by simply observing **NATURE**."

"You mean the trees, rivers and mountains have lessons they can teach?" questioned Declan.

"Absolutely," confirmed Dad. "Let's take those three things in **NATURE** and see what lessons they provide."

"Okay," acknowledged Sophie. "Let's start with trees."

"Trees offer many lessons," stated Mom. "Let's focus on the seed. Each tree has thousands of seeds that it drops every year. Some of the seeds land on rock and don't take root. Some seeds are snatched up by the birds and squirrels. Other seeds begin to take root but become overgrown by weeds and do not make it into a tree."

"There are many **OBSTACLES** that the successful seed must overcome to become a mighty tree," Dad added. "Like a tree's seeds, our **THOUGHTS** are plentiful. In order for our **THOUGHTS** to turn into a grand tree that lives for hundreds of years, we must be careful on how we tend to our **THOUGHTS**. We must carry ourselves with a positive **ATTITUDE** and **BELIEVE** in ourselves. This provides fertile soil for the **THOUGHT** of our **DREAM** to take root and flourish like the acorn that transforms into a mighty oak tree."

"When I look at a tree now, I'll think of how it was once a seed that had a **DREAM** of becoming a tree. I will remember that each tree had a positive **ATTITUDE** and **BELIEVED** in itself as it transformed," explained Sophie.

"Why aren't all trees big and mighty?" inquired Declan.

"Well, some seeds were given bigger **THOUGHTS** and **DREAMS**," described Mom. "Unlike a seed, that is destined to either be an oak, maple, pine or something else, you have the ability to **CHOOSE** any **DREAM** you want."

"I want my **DREAM** to be a mighty oak tree!" shouted Sophie.

"That's neat," spoke Declan. "How does **NATURE** provide **EDUCATION** through rivers and mountains?"

"Okay, let's look at the river. Have you kids seen pictures of the Grand Canyon?"

"Yes, I have Dad," mentioned Sophie. "I learned in school that over thousands of years, the river has eroded the rock and formed the Grand Canyon."

"Precisely," affirmed Mom. "Let me ask you, when you think of water and rock, which one do you think of as being stronger?"

"Definitely the rock," declared Declan.

"Most people do," noted Mom. "Water flowing up against rock will be deflected due to the strength of the rock. Over time, the river has unwavering **PRESISTENCE.** The water is able to cut away at the rock and carve a Grand Canyon."

"That's a lot of **PERSISTENCE,**" responded Declan.

"Think of how much **PERSISTENCE** the little acorn seed had to have to go from being stuck in the mud, to being a tiny tree and surviving winter after winter," assured Dad.

"That's a lot of **PERSISTENCE,**" repeated Declan.

"Now what about the mountain?" asked Sophie. "What lesson does the mountain teach us?"

"If you're trying to climb to the top of the mountain, do you think that would be easy or difficult?" questioned Mom.

"Very difficult," shouted Declan.

"I see," nodded Sophie. "It takes a lot of **PERSISTENCE** to climb the mountain."

"That's right," asserted Mom. "The larger your **DREAM,** the more **PERSISTENCE** you'll need."

"The higher the mountain, the better the view," claimed Dad. "The bigger the **DREAM,** the more **OBSTACLES** you'll face which will require more **PERSISTENCE** to overcome. The bigger the **DREAM,** the bigger the reward when you achieve it."

"Wow!" gushed Sophie. "I didn't realize how many lessons you could learn from **NATURE.**"

"These are just the tip of the iceberg," Mom pointed out. "An iceberg offers a wonderful example of **WORK**. I think you two have had enough for one morning."

"This morning I'm feeling like a bowl of fruit. Afterall, it's **NATURE'S** breakfast!" emphasized Dad.

CHAPTER 15

O is for OBSTACLE

The following Sunday morning, Mom and Dad came down the steps to coffee, toast, and a bowl of fruit.

"Okay," grinned Dad. "We need to start making these daily lessons!"

"Thank you, kids!" gushed Mom. "You know you don't have to do this every Sunday morning."

"We know," replied Sophie. "We **LOVE** you guys so much and want to show you our **GRATITUDE** for being our parents and providing this fun **EDUCATION**."

"We want to be **KIND** and **HELPFUL**," added Declan.

"Okay," said Dad. "Who's turn is it to go to the chalk board?"

"My turn," volunteered Sophie.

> "Have a positive **ATTITUDE!**
> **BELIEFS** lead to achievements!
> Make good **CHOICES!**
> Chase your **DREAMS!**
> **EDUCATION** does not end at school!
> **FORGIVENESS** to all others!
> Always give **GRATITUDE!**
> Give **HELP** to those in need!

> **INTEGRITY** is doing the right thing, even when no one is looking!
> Smile with **JOY!**
> **Always** show KINDNESS!
> **LOVE** always!
> **MISTAKES** are hidden lessons!
> Learn from **NATURE!**
> **'O!'**..."

"I know this one," asserted Declan. "'O' is for **OBSTACLE.**"

"Very good Declan," praised Mom. "You have been paying attention."

"You guys keep talking about being in an **OBSTACLE** maze course. Plus, last week, we talked about the **OBSTACLE** of climbing a mountain."

"Exactly," remarked Mom. "Think of **OBSTACLES** as being the gate that keeps most people from completing the maze and achieving their **DREAMS**. Some **OBSTACLES** are certainly more challenging than others. Just know that if you **BELIEVE** in yourself and **CHOOSE** not to give up, it's only a matter of time until you will master the **OBSTACLE** and move another step closer to your **DREAM.**"

"That's right," agreed Dad. "Not only are **OBSTACLES** necessary gates on your **OBSTACLE** maze course, but you actually shouldn't mind if your **DREAMS** are behind a lot of **OBSTACLES.**"

"Because they make you stronger?" questioned Declan.

"Exactly," confirmed Dad. "Each time you overcome an **OBSTACLE**, you'll develop a stronger **ATTITUDE** and have more **BELIEF** in yourself which will better prepare you for the next **OBSTACLE**."

"That's sort of like working out, isn't it?" asked Sophie.

"It's exactly like working out," remarked Mom. "Each workout presents an **OBSTACLE,** whether it's a two-mile run or lifting weights. After each workout, with the proper nutrients and rest, your muscles will recover and grow stronger."

"So, the only way to get stronger or become a better runner is to put in the **WORK** and overcome one **OBSTACLE** at a time?" asked Declan.

"That is true with achieving any **DREAM,**" declared Dad. "It takes **WORK** and **PERSISTANCE** to overcome either a big **OBSTACLE** or a series of **OBSTACLES**."

"Or, a series of big **OBSTACLES!**" shouted Sophie.

"If you **CHOOSE** to keep **PERSISTANT** and keep **WORKING**, you will eventually overcome even a series of big **OBSTACLES**. The more challenging the **OBSTACLES**, the more **JOY** you will experience when you ultimately achieve your **DREAM,**" described Dad.

"Just like you say Dad," responded Declan. "The higher the climb, the better the view!"

"Precisely," proclaimed Dad. "Little, easy goals might be easy, but where is the **JOY** and satisfaction in that? Close your eyes and pretend that you each just climbed a three-foot hill. Would you be excited, inspired and filled with **JOY**?"

"Dad don't be silly. Of course not," realized Sophie.

"However, what if you climbed a 10,000-foot mountain that overlooked lakes, rivers and valleys that could be seen for miles upon miles?" Dad continued. "Wouldn't you feel very proud and much happier?"

"Of course, we would," admitted Declan. "That view would be incredible."

"Now let me let you two in on a secret," whispered Dad. "The **JOY** and satisfaction are equal to the amount of **WORK** you put in to overcome the **OBSTACLES**. If you don't believe me, why wouldn't you have that same since of **JOY** if I were to just take a picture and show you that same view."

"I never thought of it like that before," said Sophie. "In our journey through our **OBSTACLE** maze course, we shouldn't be discouraged when we come up against an **OBSTACLE.** We should maintain a positive **ATTITUDE** and think to ourselves how much more **JOY** we will have when we finally reach our **DREAM**."

"That's exactly right," assured Mom. "Knowing that will help you keep that positive **ATTITUDE** and will give you the strength to keep **PERSISTENT** through your **OBSTACLE** maze course."

Sophie looked at Declan and boasted, "Stay **PERSISTENT** and do not give up in your **OBSTACLE** maze."

Declan smiled confidently, "I have a feeling that I know what next week's word will be."

"Maybe you do," recognized Dad. "However, for now the **OBSTACLE** in front of you is beating me to the last muffin."

CHAPTER 16

P is for PERSISTENCE

The following Sunday, as Mom and Dad came down the steps, they were each greeted with a cup of coffee, toast, a bowl of fruit and eggs in a skillet.

"Amazing." smiled Mom. "Let me cook the eggs, I don't want you two to burn yourselves."

"We won't," replied Sophie. "Besides, this is how we learn. If they don't come out perfect, we'll learn from our **MISTAKE** and get better next time. Besides we want to conquer this **OBSTACLE**."

"Just be careful and don't burn yourselves," warned Mom.

"I won't," replied Sophie again.

"Very well then," Mom acknowledged. "Okay Declan, your turn to go to the chalk board."

"Yes!" exclaimed Declan. "I love going to the chalk board.

> Have a positive **ATTITUDE!**
> **BELIEFS** lead to achievements!
> Make good **CHOICES!**
> Chase your **DREAMS!**
> **EDUCATION** does not end at school!

FORGIVENESS to all others!

Always give **GRATITUDE!**

Give **HELP** to those in need!

INTEGRITY is doing the right thing, even when no one is looking!

Smile with **JOY!**

Always show **KINDNESS!**

LOVE always!

MISTAKES are hidden lessons!

Learn from **NATURE!**

OBSTACLES are necessary and make the reward sweeter!

'**P!**'..."

"'P' is for **PERSISTENCE**," continued Sophie.

"Very good. Well done," praised Mom.

"Yep, we talked about needing **PERSISTENCE** to overcome the **OBSTACLES** we'll face in our maze. I remember how **NATURE** teaches **PERSISTENCE** through seeds becoming large trees. This is also true for a river forming the Grand Canyon. Likewise, **PERSISTENCE** is needed in order to climb a 10,000- foot mountain," described Sophie.

I guess last week's lesson was a two for one," smiled Dad.

"That's okay," Mom confirmed. "This is one of the more important principles you need to master in order to achieve your **DREAMS**. Especially in today's world where you can get almost anything instantly, the discipline of patience is becoming more and more rare."

"Mom's right," affirmed Dad. "Most people want the easy road. They want the quickest, easiest path. If something looks difficult or looks like it will take a long time, most people haven't worked to develop their **PERSISTENCE** muscle. They either give up at the first **OBSTACLE,** or never begin on the path towards a difficult **DREAM**."

"That's sad," sighed Declan. "Don't they know that every **DREAM** requires going through an **OBSTACLE** maze course. The bigger the **DREAM**, the bigger and longer the **OBSTACLE** maze course will be."

"At the starting line, most people peak their heads in and see the first **OBSTACLE** in the maze course. They immediately start thinking of all of the negative reasons of why they won't be able to complete the course," relayed Mom. "They haven't worked to develop a positive **ATTITUDE.** They haven't been taught the importance of **BELIEVING** in themselves and making good **CHOICES.** The **THOUGHT** of staying **PERSISTENT** and overcoming every **OBSTACLE** along the way, becomes overwhelming and they quit or don't begin."

"Unfortunately, some kids haven't been taught to always carry themselves with high **INTEGRITY.** They see if they can cheat by skipping certain **OBSTACLES.** Eventually they are always caught and sent further back," added Dad.

"Cheating never pays!" shouted Declan.

"Now, you two understand that not only are

OBSTACLES a necessary part of the maze, but the more **OBSTACLES** there are and the bigger they are, the more **JOY** you will experience along your journey. Ultimately you will finally achieve your **DREAM**," promised Mom. "Knowing that, **HELPS** you keep that positive mental **ATTITUDE** which will ultimately **HELP** you keep your **PERSISTENCE** on your journey."

"If you don't believe us on how important **PERSISTENCE** is, look at what Jesus said," added Dad.

"I tell you, keep asking and it will be given to you. Keep seeking and you will find. Keep knocking, and it will be opened to you. For everyone who asks receives. He who seeks finds. To him who knocks it will be opened."

— *Luke 11:9-10, World English Bible*

"If you kids learn to master the skill of **PERSISTENCE**, you can master any other skill that you desire," said Mom.

"All we have to do is not give up?" asked Declan.

"Exactly," nodded Mom. "Like all of the other keys, it may be simple, but it requires great discipline."

"We can summarize **PERSISTENCE** as never giving up," defined Sophie.

"Bingo!" cheered Dad. "Never **QUIT**."

"Now I'm going to keep my **PERSISTENCE** and finish all of my breakfast," Dad said with a big smile on his face.

CHAPTER 17

Q is for Never Quit

The following Sunday, Mom and Dad came down the steps to see a full breakfast. Waiting for them was coffee, toast, a bowl of fruit, eggs, and sausage.

"Does it get any better than this?" Dad asked Mom.

"I don't think so," replied Mom. "Look they even have cleaned up after themselves. Very impressive kids."

"Look Dad," pointed Sophie. "Since I know how much you love Mom's Thanksgiving stuffing, I put the leftovers in the eggs."

"I think I'm going to cry," laughed Dad. "These are going to be the best eggs ever!"

"Excuse me," interrupted Mom.

"Next to yours of course," Dad remarked.

"Okay Sophie," motioned Mom. "Your turn to the chalk board."

"Have a positive **ATTITUDE!**
BELIEFS lead to achievements!
Make good **CHOICES!**
Chase your **DREAMS!**
EDUCATION does not end at school!
FORGIVENESS to all others!

Always give **GRATITUDE**!
Give **HELP** to those in need!
INTEGRITY is doing the right thing, even when no one is looking!
Smile with **JOY**!
Always show **KINDNESS**!
LOVE always!
MISTAKES are hidden lessons!
Learn from **NATURE**!
OBSTACLES are necessary and make the reward sweeter!
PERSISTENCE is never giving up!
'Q!'...

This one is going to be tricky," murmured Sophie. "What important word begins with Q?"

"You're right," acknowledged Mom. "Q is tricky. In fact, it's the only word on our list that is what **NOT** to do."

"Then it must be **QUIT**!" announced Sophie.

"Right again," confirmed Dad. "**NEVER QUIT**. This message is so important, that you kids are hearing it two weeks in a row. **NEVER QUIT** is the same as keeping **PERSISTENCE**."

"We learned this last week," remembered Declan.

"Let's look at a real-life story to help show how important it is to **NEVER QUIT**," persuaded Mom. "This is a story of a person who simply would not give up..."

This person failed in business in 1831.

He then was defeated for state legislature in 1832.

He failed again in another business in 1833.

He lost his fiancée in 1835.

He suffered from a nervous breakdown in 1836.

He ran for congress and was defeated in 1843 and again in 1848.

In 1855 he tried to run for Senate and was again defeated.

The following year in 1856 he ran for vice-president and lost.

So, in 1859, he tried running for Senate again, and lost again.

Others would have **QUIT** years earlier, but not this man. For this man **NEVER QUIT**, and in 1860, Abraham Lincoln became the 16th President of the United States of America."

"That's amazing," shouted Sophie. "I wonder what it would be like today, if Mr. Lincoln would have given up and not became the President of the United States."

"Thankfully, we don't have to know what that would be like," spoke Dad. "Always remember, the difference between some of history's most amazing achievements and biggest failures is the will to **PERSERVERE** and **NEVER QUIT**."

"No matter what the outcome, if you give your best and **NEVER QUIT**, you can always be very proud of yourself" added Mom. "For you did not give in to the temptation of **QUITING**."

"Wow!" exclaimed Declan. "I understand why we spent two weeks in a row on **PERSISTENCE** and **NOT QUITING**. In our **OBSTACLE** maze course, if we want to make it to the end and achieve our **DREAMS**, we must be determined to **NEVER QUIT** and always **PERSERVERE** through the tough times."

"Keeping a positive **ATTITUDE** and **BELIEVING** in ourselves will help us **PERSERVERE** and **NOT QUIT**" mentioned Sophie.

"Exactly," nodded Dad. "Remember, don't be disappointed or surprised when you come up on **OBSTACLES**. It's simply part of the game. There will be many. That's okay, because you two know that the more **OBSTACLES** there are, the more **JOY** you will have on your journey."

"I'm going to try and teach you kids by example," continued Dad. "While it may be difficult to eat this full plate of food... I accept my **RESPONSIBILITY**!"

CHAPTER 18

R is for RESPONSIBILITY

The following Sunday, Mom and Dad came down the stairs to a super complete and healthy breakfast, which became the new normal.

"This never gets old kids," said Dad. "We appreciate your **KINDNESS**. This is a real treat."

"Awe, it's nothing," replied Sophie.

"My turn to go to the chalk board," shouted Declan.

"Okay," agreed Mom. "Let us at least grab our cup of coffee first."

"Have a positive **ATTITUDE!**
BELIEFS lead to achievements!
Make good **CHOICES!**
Chase your **DREAMS!**
EDUCATION does not end at school!
FORGIVENESS to all others!
Always give **GRATITUDE!**
Give **HELP** to those in need!
INTEGRITY is doing the right thing, even when no one is looking!
Smile with **JOY!**
Always show **KINDNESS!**

LOVE always!

MISTAKES are hidden lessons!

Learn from **NATURE**!

OBSTACLES are necessary and make the reward sweeter!

PERSISTENCE is never giving up!

NEVER be a **QUITTER**!

'R!'…

Hmm," thought Declan. "Is it rest?"

"No," responded Mom. "However, getting your rest every day is very important."

"Yeah Buddy," added Dad. "If you want to grow up to be *almost* as strong as me, you're going to need plenty of rest!"

"Funny Dad," laughed Declan. "Just wait until I'm in high school."

"Okay, okay," sighed Mom. "Sophie, do you have any guesses?"

"Respect," asserted Sophie.

"That's a great guess," commented Mom. "Respect is extremely important. You are showing respect when you carry yourself with **INTEGRITY**, are **KIND** to others, **HELP** others and **LOVE** others."

"Also, you show respect when you **FORGIVE** others and express your **GRATITUDE**," explained Sophie.

"Okay," acknowledged Declan. "We're ready, just tell us."

"You're not **QUITING** already, are you?" questioned Dad.

"No," answered Declan. "Now we are ready to continue with our **EDUCATION**."

"Wow, great answer," confirmed Mom. "Okay, R is for **RESPONSIBILITY**."

"Like we're **RESPONSIBLE** for making our beds each morning?" wondered Sophie.

"That's right," affirmed Dad. "Now what happens if your bed does not get made in the morning?"

"I'll have a messy bed when I go back to bed at night," shrugged Sophie.

"Who would be **RESPONSIBLE** for that?" inquired Mom.

"Sophie would be," nodded Declan.

"What if Sophie overslept and didn't have time to make the bed, because she risked missing the bus?" Mom questioned.

"Yeah!" shouted Sophie. "That wouldn't be my fault. You should have woken me up sooner."

"Here's the problem with taking that position," spoke Dad. "What if your mom is busy making lunches, getting your brother ready, scheduling doctors' appointments and checking about soccer practice and piano lessons."

"Wow, that's a lot of stuff to take care of," Sophie chimed.

"That's right," stated Dad. "Your Mother has a lot of **RESPONSIBILITIES**. If she can't get to everything, she doesn't point the finger at someone or something else. You see, if she were to do that, then she would be giving up her control of the outcome. When people place blame on someone or something else, they are giving up and saying that they cannot control the outcome. Remember, in your **OBSTACLE** maze course, there will be many dead-end alleys, and difficult **OBSTACLES**, but always accept full **RESPONSIBILITY**. When something doesn't go your way, ask yourself what you have learned and what you can do different next time to have a better outcome."

"Those that learn to always accept **RESPONSIBILITY** for both positive and negative outcomes, will learn more quickly from **MISTAKES** that are guaranteed to appear along the maze," added Mom. "The quicker you can learn from your **MISTAKES**, the quicker you can overcome the **OBSTACLE** and move that much closer to achieving your **DREAM**."

"This will also help you keep a positive **ATTITUDE**. Rather than looking to assign blame for the **MISTAKE**, by accepting **RESPONSIBILITY**, you are immediately looking to correct and move on," described Dad.

"Take **RESPONSIBILITY** and don't make excuses," proclaimed Declan.

"Couldn't have said it any better," admitted Mom.

"Now I'm going to take **RESPONSIBILITY** of making sure we all get to enjoy a hot breakfast," smiled Dad. "We'll **SEARCH** for the new word next week," Dad insisted.

CHAPTER 19

S is for SEEK

The following Sunday, Mom and Dad came down the stairs, to another hot breakfast and hot coffee. As they each grabbed their cups of coffee, Sophie was at the chalk board.

"It's my turn," Sophie said.

"Have a positive **ATTITUDE!**
BELIEFS lead to achievements!
Make good **CHOICES!**
Chase your **DREAMS!**
EDUCATION does not end at school!
FORGIVENESS to all others!
Always give **GRATITUDE!**
Give **HELP** to those in need!
INTEGRITY is doing the right thing, even when no one is looking!
Smile with **JOY!**
Always show **KINDNESS!**
LOVE always!
MISTAKES are hidden lessons!
Learn from **NATURE!**

OBSTACLES are necessary and make the reward sweeter!

PERSISTENCE is never giving up!

NEVER be a **QUITTER!**

Always accept **RESPONSIBILITY!**

'S!'...

'S' is for SOPHIE!" exclaimed Sophie.

"Well, that is definitely our favorite word that begins with 'S,'" acknowledged Dad. "However, that's not the secret word."

"Success!" shouted Declan.

"Great guess," assured Mom. "This word when applied with **PERSISTANCE** will lead to success."

"Okay, what is the word for the letter 'S?'" wondered Sophie.

"'S' is for **SEARCH**," answered Mom.

"Like hide and go seek?" asked Declan.

"Correct," nodded Dad. "That is a great way to think about it. Imagine your **DREAMS** are hiding at the end of your **OBSTACLE** maze course and the only way you're going to find your **DREAMS** is by **SEEKING** with **PERSISTENCE**."

"So, don't give up even though it may be difficult to find," added Sophie.

"Exactly," confirmed Mom. "You both have learned how important **PERSISTENCE** is in obtaining your **DREAMS**. Equally important as **PERSISTANCE** is active

SEEKING. No matter how **PERSISTENT** you are, if you are only sitting down and not actively **SEEKING** after your **DREAMS**, how likely will you be in obtaining them?"

"Not very likely at all," shrugged Sophie.

"You must **BELIEVE** you can find your **DREAMS** and **SEEK** with a positive **ATTITUDE**," stated Declan.

"Yeah," agreed Sophie. "When you go down the wrong path in the maze, you have to accept **RESPONSIBILITY** and learn from your **MISTAKE**."

"You kids are really picking this up," affirmed Dad. "What about those you meet along the maze. How can you gain their **HELP** along the way?"

"By being **KIND** and **HELPING** others when they need it," responded Sophie.

"Even if someone sends you down the wrong direction, you should always **LOVE** others and **FORGIVE** those who were mean to you," spoke Declan.

"Very good," gushed Mom. "We're proud of you two. You're starting to see how these keys all come together. They will not only **HELP** you achieve your **DREAMS** but will allow you to **HELP** others on their journeys as well."

"Now back to the importance of **SEEKING**," directed Dad. "**SEEKING** is the beginning action steps needed to ultimately find your **DREAMS**. You can see this from the **OBSTACLE** maze course. Also, look at what Jesus says about **SEEKING**:

*Ask and it will be given to you; **SEEK** and you will find; knock and the door will be opened to you.*

"**BELIEVE** that breadcrumb clues will be provided to you along the way. Only if you **SEEK** with **PERSISTENCE,**" concluded Mom.

"Now that is a comforting **THOUGHT,**" smiled Dad. "**BELIEVING** that breadcrumb clues will be provided to those who implement daily the keys that you kids have been learning about. That takes the fear out of the game and makes the journey exciting."

"These Sunday morning lessons are my favorite **EDUCATION!**" cried Sophie.

"I'm glad you kids are having **JOY** with these lessons," praised Mom.

"Me too," boasted Dad. "Now pardon me, while I **SEEK** after some syrup!"

CHAPTER 20

T is for THINK

The following Sunday morning, Mom and Dad came to their usual Sunday breakfast.

"Here is your coffee," said Declan.

"Thank you, kind sir," replied Dad.

"Wonder what we should talk about this morning?" wondered Mom.

"You know," chimed Sophie. "It's time for our **EDUCATION** on the building blocks to success."

"Okay!" exclaimed Mom. "Whose turn is it to go to the chalk board?"

"It's my turn today!" shouted Declan.

> "Have a positive **ATTITUDE!**
> **BELIEFS** lead to achievements!
> Make good **CHOICES!**
> Chase your **DREAMS!**
> **EDUCATION** does not end at school!
> **FORGIVENESS** to all others!
> Always give **GRATITUDE!**
> Give **HELP** to those in need!
> **INTEGRITY** is doing the right thing, even when no one is looking!

Smile with **JOY!**

Always show **KINDNESS!**

LOVE always!

MISTAKES are hidden lessons!

Learn from **NATURE!**

OBSTACLES are necessary and make the reward sweeter!

PERSISTENCE is never giving up!

NEVER be a **QUITTER!**

Always accept **RESPONSIBILITY!**

Seek and you will find!

'T!'…

I know this one," laughed Declan. "'T' is for truck!"

"Nice thought, but keep **THINKING,**" insisted Dad.

"Is 'T' for teach?" questioned Sophie.

"That's a good word," acknowledged Mom. "It's good to be able to teach others when you're ready and you can provide guidance. However, teach is not our building block word for the letter 'T.'"

"Hmmm," murmured Declan.

"You can get it," assured Mom. "Just keep **THINKING.**"

"If you **THINK** long enough, I'm sure you'll **THINK** of the word," added Dad.

"Is it **THINK?**" inquired Sophie.

"Bingo!" Dad pointed out. "**THINKING** is one of the most important building blocks for your foundation. In fact, **THINKING** is one of the cornerstones of all the building blocks."

"What do you mean by cornerstone?" questioned Declan.

"**THINK** of each of these building block words as important blocks that hold up the building that you are creating. The building ultimately represents the achievements of your **DREAMS**. To build a grand building or even a skyscraper, you need to have a strong foundation. This foundation will hold the building up day and night, no matter how strong the storms, or how long and cold the winters are. To do that, requires a strong foundation. That is what your mom and I have been teaching you two over the past several months. We have been teaching you those vital characteristics, that will support you two on your journey through your own **OBSTACLE** maze course."

"I like that thought," complimented Sophie. "So, if **THINK** is an important cornerstone, what words are the other cornerstone words?"

"Why don't we finish revealing all of the building blocks through the letter Z and then we can recap and identify the cornerstone words," suggested Mom.

"Okay," agreed Sophie. "I just don't get why **THINKING** is so important. I **THINK** all the time."

"That's right," remarked Mom. "We all do. You must realize that you control what you **THINK** about. The difference between those who have achieved their biggest

DREAMS and those who barely get by, are the thoughts that they **THINK** about."

"That's it. Just by what they **THINK** about?" inquired Declan. "So why doesn't everyone **THINK** about being great and achieving their **DREAMS?**"

"That's a great question," affirmed Dad. "Most people haven't been taught how important their thoughts are. Most people simply don't **BELIEVE** how critically important their thoughts are."

"Let's go back to our **NATURE** example," spoke Mom. "Do you remember some of the lessons you can learn through **NATURE?**"

"Oh yeah," recalled Sophie. "I remember we learned that our thoughts are like seeds. What we **THINK** about can eventually grow into a majestic oak tree."

"That's right," smiled Mom. "Just as bountiful as there are seeds in a forest, are the thoughts in your mind. If you don't harness the power of your thoughts, they'll form based on your environment. You don't want to just leave it up to chance on what seeds sprout."

"That's right," winked Dad. "What happens when we go too long without taking care of our flower bed?"

"It grows weeds," answered Declan.

"Exactly," said Dad. "If you don't deliberately plant the types of flowers that you want to grow, then not only will your **DREAM** flowers not grow, but nasty weeds will likely grow in their place. You see, just as **NATURE'S** life cycle begins with seeds, so too does your **DREAM** achievements. Your **DREAM** seeds are your thoughts."

"Remember," guided Mom. "Your mind will have weed thoughts too, but you must let those thoughts go and focus on your beautiful **DREAM** flowers. Focusing your attention to a thought is the act of **THINKING**. While some thoughts seem to appear randomly out of thin air, you are always in control of which thoughts you give focused attention to. The focused attention, **THINKING**, is what gives the seed the necessary nutrients to grow. So, place your positive **THINKING** around your beautiful **DREAM** flowers and don't **THINK** about the weed seeds.

"Well said," praised Dad. "I can't wait to see what kind of **DREAM** flowers you two grow. Just **THINK**, I bet they will be so **UNIQUE** that the world has never seen such flowers! Now until then, I **THINK** it's time for one more pancake!"

CHAPTER 21

U is for UNIQUE

The following Sunday, Mom and Dad came downstairs to another spectacular breakfast and hot coffee.

"It doesn't get any better than this," Dad said to the kids.

"It's the least we can do for the **LOVE** and **EDUCATION** that you and Mom have been giving us," replied Sophie. "Now, if you're ready, it's my turn to the chalk board," Sophie continued.

> "Have a positive **ATTITUDE!**
> **BELIEFS** lead to achievements!
> Make good **CHOICES!**
> Chase your **DREAMS!**
> **EDUCATION** does not end at school!
> **FORGIVENESS** to all others!
> Always give **GRATITUDE!**
> Give **HELP** to those in need!
> **INTEGRITY** is doing the right thing, even
> when no one is looking!
> Smile with **JOY!**
> Always show **KINDNESS!**
> **LOVE** always!

MISTAKES are hidden lessons!

Learn from **NATURE!**

OBSTACLES are necessary and make the reward sweeter!

PERSISTENCE is never giving up!

NEVER be a **QUITTER!**

Always accept **RESPONSIBILITY!**

SEEK and you will find!

We become what we **THINK** about!

'U!'...

I know it's not unicorn, but that would be awesome," remarked Sophie.

"No, it's not a unicorn," laughed Mom. "However, it's as **UNIQUE** as a unicorn."

"What about a poke-a-dotted umbrella?" asked Declan.

"Try again," insisted Dad. "Think of something more **UNIQUE** than a poke-a-dotted umbrella.

"I know!" shouted Sophie. "A unicycle!"

"Great guess, that is **UNIQUE**, but not **UNIQUE** enough," stated Mom.

"Okay. Just tell us," pleaded Declan.

"'U' is for **UNIQUENESS**," announced Dad.

"Hey!" exclaimed Sophie. "That was tricky! Now what is so important about **UNIQUENESS**," Sophie asked?

"Let's think about it," guided Mom. "Are you aware what is special about each of your thumb prints?"

"That's how they catch bad guys," answered Declan.

"That's right," responded Mom. "Why can the police catch bad guys from thumbprints?"

"Because each person's thumbprint is different," interjected Sophie. "There are no two thumbprints alike."

"Precisely," acknowledged Mom. "Everyone's thumbprints are **UNIQUE**."

"That's just your thumbs," added Dad. "If your thumbprints are different than everyone else in the world, just think how different you are from everyone else. Just think how **UNIQUE** you are."

"Wow!" shouted Declan. "You mean there is not another person in the world just like me?"

"Not a one," spoke Mom.

"What about all the people who came before us?" inquired Sophie.

"Go back through all of the history books in all of the world," grinned Dad. "You won't find a single girl or boy that are just like the two of you."

"Wow!" cheered Sophie. "We really are **UNIQUE**."

"Now if no one in this world even has thumbprints identical to either of you, how **UNIQUE** do you think your inner desire and **DREAMS** are?" questioned Mom.

"Not only are your vision of your **DREAMS UNIQUE**, but also the paths you will take in your **OBSTACLE** maze course to reach your **DREAMS** are **UNIQUE**," added Dad. "So, it is important to remember, that your imagination will lead you down different paths than others in pursuit of your personal **DREAMS**. Never let anyone else discourage you from your **UNIQUE** paths taken to your **UNIQUE DREAMS**. Sure, it is okay to **SEEK** guidance along the way. Never be discouraged from those who do not share the same **DREAMS** as you."

"That's right," agreed Mom. "There are infinite variations to all of the **UNIQUE DREAMS**, and there are other infinite ways to reach your **DREAMS**. Cherish your imagination, and your own **UNIQUENESS**. Also remember, if someone is not **HELPING** you and encouraging you along your journey, they do not deserve your time and attention."

"Unfortunately, there will be many along your life journey who will not be of **HELP**," asserted Dad. "In fact, they will be trying to hold you back to keep you with them. Many people have fallen victims to the twenty-six traps that appear on your journey towards their **DREAMS**."

"You mean like **OBSTACLES?**" asked Declan.

"You can think of these as **OBSTACLES**," affirmed Dad. "Focus on the building blocks that you have learned and they will arm you against these **OBSTACLES**."

"What kind of **OBSTACLES** will there be?" questioned Sophie. "How will we remember all of them?"

"Lucky for you two, if you can remember your alphabet, you'll be well prepared to remember these twenty-six enemies that will test you and try and prevent you from achieving your **DREAMS**."

Sophie looked over at Declan with a smile. "Does this

mean we have more **EDUCATION** after we finish with the letter Z?"

"Remember Sophie, **EDUCATION** is something you should pursue your entire life. It does not simply begin and end in the classroom," smiled Mom.

"So that means, we'll get more lessons?" inquired Declan.

"After we get through the twenty-six building blocks from which you can build massive skyscraper **DREAMS**, we'll teach you about the twenty-six enemies that you need to guard against. For these twenty-six enemies will be looking for the weak spot in your buildings and will try and to prevent you from building your skyscraper, and even try to take it down after you've built it."

"I don't like those enemies already," admitted Sophie.

"Now don't get too worked up yet," warned Mom. "By the time we get to Z with the building blocks, you two will have sufficient **VALOR** to take on even the biggest enemy."

"**VALOR?**" asked Declan. "What is **VALOR?**"

"We'll get there," promised Dad. "For now, I think I'll have my pancake **UNIQUE**. I'll have mine with whip cream on it!"

CHAPTER 22

V is for VALOR

The following Sunday, Mom and Dad came down the stairs once again to a large breakfast.

"This is better than breakfast in bed," grinned Dad.

"Look Mom and Dad," said Sophie. "We made heart shaped pancakes."

"Very impressive," complimented Mom. "I'll have an extra pancake since they're hearts."

"Okay! Whose turn is it today to read from the chalk board?" Dad asked.

"It's my turn!" shouted Declan.

"Have a positive **ATTITUDE!**
BELIEFS lead to achievements!
Make good **CHOICES!**
Chase your **DREAMS!**
EDUCATION does not end at school!
FORGIVENESS to all others!
Always give **GRATITUDE!**
Give **HELP** to those in need!
INTEGRITY is doing the right thing, even when no one is looking!
Smile with **JOY!**

Always show **KINDNESS!**
LOVE always!
MISTAKES are hidden lessons!
Learn from **NATURE!**
OBSTACLES are necessary and make the
reward sweeter!
PERSISTENCE is never giving up!
NEVER be a **QUITTER!**
Always accept **RESPONSIBILITY!**
SEEK and you will find!
We become what we **THINK** about!
UNIQUENESS is special!
'V!'...

'V' is for victory," continued Declan.

"Good guess, but no soup. Guess again," spoke Mom.

"'V' is for vacuum," laughed Sophie.

"That's right," replied Dad. "How did you figure that out?"

"It is? I was just joking," admitted Sophie.

"So was I," laughed Dad.

"Okay, 'V' is for **VALOR,**" stated Mom.

"Oh yeah, I remember you saying that word last week," recalled Declan. "What does **VALOR** mean?"

"From the Merriam-Webster dictionary, **VALOR** is defined as strength of mind or spirit that enables a person to encounter danger with firmness," affirmed Dad. "**VALOR** is personal bravery."

"Why is it important to be brave?" questioned Sophie. "We're not going to have to face bad guys, will we?"

"Not necessarily bad guys," remarked Mom. "Remember, there are many enemies and traps along your **OBSTACLE** maze course that will try and hold you back from reaching your **DREAMS**. In order to make it through your very own **UNIQUE OBSTACLE** maze course, you must keep **PERSISTENT** with your **VALOR**. Some **OBSTACLES** will seem scary and a voice in your head will be trying to keep you from continuing. **CHOOSE VALOR** and trust the other inner voice in your head that reminds yourself that you are simply facing another necessary **OBSTACLE** on your way to the amazing **DREAM**."

"I want to be brave like a knight," asserted Declan.

"That's a good way to vision yourself going through the **OBSTACLE** maze course," praised Dad. "The armor, shield and sword are the important lessons that your mom and I have been teaching you. This will help protect your mind, body and spirit on your journey. Trust the most powerful protective force shield that you have, is the magic cloak of **BELIEVING**. When you truly **BELIEVE** in yourselves and know that the only way you will not achieve your **DREAMS** is if you give up, you will always find your **VALOR** and press forward."

"I think only boys are knights," sighed Sophie. "Can girls have **VALOR**?"

"Are you kidding?" inquired Dad. "Your Mother is the bravest person I know. Of course, girls are **VALIENT**."

"Sophie, just look at every Disney princess," added Mom. "Every single one of them had to overcome their own **OBSTACLES** in pursuit of their **DREAMS**. Every single one of them had a **CHOICE** to make. Each princess had to decide whether she was going to give up, or be **VALIENT**, **BELIEVE** in her **DREAMS** and pursue them with complete **PERSISTENCE**."

"Moana pursued her **DREAM** of traveling over the dangerous water. She had to summon up a lot of courage to chase her **DREAM**," described Dad. "What about the movie Brave?"

"That's right!" cheered Sophie. "Girls really are **VALIENT**."

"Absolutely," agreed Mom. "It doesn't matter what your gender is. There will come a time in everyone's own journey where he or she is faced with an **OBSTACLE** that seems insurmountable. Unfortunately, most people will not even attempt the **OBSTACLE**. However, you two now understand that your **BELIEF** in yourselves, provide you with superpowers that will protect you. These superpowers will also help you get by whatever **OBSTACLE** is in the way, no matter how big and scary it may seem."

"That's right," guaranteed Dad. "It may take some **WORK**, but trust that you will get through. Always remember, your **UNIQUE DREAM** is waiting for you to claim it."

"Hey Dad," whispered Declan.

"Yes Buddy," answered Dad.

"What's that?" Declan said as he pointed behind his dad.

As Dad looked behind him, Declan snatched his last pancake.

"My **DREAM** was the last pancake," declared Declan. "I decided to be **VALIENT** and overcome the **OBSTACLE**."

"Wow!" said Dad. "I'm proud of your **VALOR**, but now you better run!"

CHAPTER 23

W is for WORK

The following Sunday, Mom and Dad came down the stairs to another good breakfast.

"I can't believe we're already up to the letter 'W,'" said Dad. "Good thing we have another twenty-six lessons to teach after we get through to Z."

"That's right," agreed Sophie. "After the building blocks, we're going to learn about all of the traps."

"Sure thing," grinned Mom. "Why don't we see what today's lesson is about. Who's turn is it to the chalkboard?"

"It's my turn!" exclaimed Sophie.

"Have a positive **ATTITUDE!**
BELIEFS lead to achievements!
Make good **CHOICES!**
Chase your **DREAMS!**
EDUCATION does not end at school!
FORGIVENESS to all others!
Always give **GRATITUDE!**
Give **HELP** to those in need!
INTEGRITY is doing the right thing, even when no one is looking!
Smile with **JOY!**

Always show **KINDNESSS!**
LOVE always!
MISTAKES are hidden lessons!
Learn from **NATURE!**
OBSTACLES are necessary and make the reward sweeter!
PERSISTENCE is never giving up!
NEVER be a **QUITTER!**
Always accept **RESPONSIBILITY!**
SEEK and you will find!
We become what we **THINK** about!
UNIQUENESS is special!
VALOR is strength of mind and spirit!
'W!'…

'W' is for women," Sophie said smiling.

"Well, as great **as** women are, it's not women," corrected Mom.

"I bet 'W' is for **WORK,**" guessed Declan.

"Impressive. That's correct," remarked Mom. "How did you know that?"

"You and Dad always tell us to **WORK** hard."

"Excellent!" praised Dad. "That's right! Good fortune comes to those who put in the **WORK**."

"Yeah, but **WORK** can be difficult and boring at times," admitted Sophie.

"That's okay," replied Mom. "If it were easy, everyone

would be **WORKING**. When you consistently **WORK**, you are building character."

"What's character?" asked Declan.

"Character is your inner self," Dad pointed out. "Through a strong **WORK** ethic, you are building a positive self-esteem. You two have learned that when you chase your **DREAMS**, there will be plenty of **OBSTACLES** on your journey. **WORKING** towards your **DREAMS** are the only way to reach them. As nice as it would seem, there will not be a helicopter that will pick up your **DREAM,** fly over the **OBSTACLE** maze course and deliver it to you on your lap."

"That sure would be nice," said Sophie.

"Maybe," spoke Mom. "The gratification you will feel when you finally accomplish your **DREAMS**, will be equal to the amount of **WORK** that you had to put in to achieve it. Remember your Dad's saying… The higher the climb, the better the view. In other words, the more **WORK** you put into something, the greater the reward."

"That's right," confirmed Dad. "Another good line I remind myself of when I am getting tired is from Ohio State's old football coach, Woody Hayes. He used to say, 'Anything easy, ain't worth a darn!'"

"He must have really liked **WORK**," stated Declan.

"Whether he liked it or not, doesn't matter. It's clear that he valued **WORK**," emphasized Dad.

"Sophie, do you remember how proud and happy

you were when you performed in your piano recital?" questioned Mom.

"Oh yes," smiled Sophie. "I was so proud. When I finished that song that I had practiced for months, I felt amazing."

"Do you remember the looks on Dad and my face?" inquired Mom.

"I sure do," recalled Sophie. "You guys were smiling and clapping. You looked very proud."

"We sure were," affirmed Mom. "We were so proud because we knew how long and how hard you **WORKED** at that song. You kept **PERSISTENCE** and didn't give up when it was difficult."

"That still makes me feel happy today," said Sophie with another big smile.

"Declan, do you remember how proud you were when you hit your first home run?" asked Dad.

"That was awesome!" cheered Declan. "We **WORKED** so hard, and it really paid off."

"Exactly," winked Dad. "How many baseballs do you think I've pitched to you before you hit that home run in the game?"

"Hundreds," said Declan.

"That sounds like you put in a lot of **WORK**," suggested Dad. "Which paid off."

"Dad," called Sophie. "Practicing the piano and baseball isn't **WORK**. It's practice."

"**WORK** is anything you are doing that gets you closer

to your goal or **DREAM**," described Mom. "So, picture that **OBSTACLE** maze course. Every step you take throughout the maze, every **OBSTACLE** that you climb, every alley you go down all lead to dead-ends. Then you must turn back around. Everything you do, **SEEKING** after your **DREAM,** takes energy and is **WORK**. So, when your friends roll their eyes and complain about **WORKING**, you two can smile and know that the only way to achieve your **DREAM** is by **WORKING** through the maze."

"Exactly," boasted Dad. "In your mind, see yourself getting by each **OBSTACLE**, one **OBSTACLE** at a time. See just beyond the **OBSTACLE**, a giant 'X', and tell yourself, that **X**-marks the spot. It might take several attempts to get past the **OBSTACLE**, but with **PERSISTENCE** and hard **WORK**, you know it's just a matter of time."

"Now my focus is on **WORKING** through the rest of these pancakes and keeping Declan away from my plate!"

CHAPTER 24

X is for X marks the spot

The following Sunday morning, Mom and Dad came downstairs to another wonderful breakfast.

"Good morning kids," said Mom.

"Good morning," both kids replied together.

Before the cups of coffee were poured, Declan was at the chalkboard ready for the week's lesson.

> "Have a positive **ATTITUDE!**
> **BELIEFS** lead to achievements!
> Make good **CHOICES!**
> Chase your **DREAMS!**
> **EDUCATION** does not end at school!
> **FORGIVENESS** to all others!
> Always give **GRATITUDE!**
> Give **HELP** to those in need!
> **INTEGRITY** is doing the right thing, even
> when no one is looking!
> Smile with **JOY!**
> Always show **KINDNESS!**
> **LOVE** always!
> **MISTAKES** are hidden lessons!
> Learn from **NATURE!**

OBSTACLES are necessary and make the reward sweeter!

PERSISTENCE is never giving up!

NEVER be a **QUITTER!**

Always accept **RESPONSIBILITY!**

SEEK and you will find!

We become what we **THINK** about!

UNIQUENESS is special!

VALOR is strength of mind and spirit!

WORK always comes before the reward!

X!...

This is a tricky one," admitted Declan.

"Yep, this is kind of tricky, because it does not stand for a word," added Dad. **"'X'-marks the spot."**

"'**X'-marks the spot** you of where you are aiming," described Mom.

"What if we're not aiming anywhere?" questioned Sophie.

"Then don't expect to hit your target," warned Mom. "You see if you don't develop the habit of setting goals, or as we refer to it here as setting the '**X' that marks the spot**, don't expect to reach them."

"Goals come in all shapes and sizes," added Dad. "Some are short-term goals, like making your bed, setting the table, or finishing your homework. Some are medium-term goals, like getting A's on your report card, mastering a song on the piano, or winning the league championship. Others are long-term goals which may include something you want to achieve 10, 20 or 30 years from now. No matter the goal, if you want to achieve it, you must **CHOOSE** the '**X' that marks the spot. BELIEVE** that you can achieve it, set forth with a positive **ATTITUDE** and always keep mighty **PERSISTANCE** along the way. If you do all these things, there is absolutely nothing that either of you two cannot achieve!"

"Setting the '**X' that marks the spot**, first will serve as a beacon that sets your direction. Also, remember, in your real-life **OBSTACLE** maze course, there will be many **MISTAKES** along the way. When you reflect to your 'X', it can help give you strength to keep **PERSISTENCE** and continue **WORKING** towards your goal," continued Mom.

"It's kind of like driving to Grammy and Poppy's lake house," recalled Sophie. "The '**X' that marks the spot** is the lake house. With that as our goal, we prepare for the trip by packing everything that we'll need to get there."

"We must also make sure we have enough gas," chimed Declan.

"That's right," remarked Sophie. "We establish our goal, or the '**X' that marks the spot**, and then we **WORK** towards that goal until we arrive."

"Exactly," confirmed Dad. "Without having the goal or setting the '**X' that marks the spot**, we would just be driving around aimlessly with no intention. If we did that, do you think we'd arrive to the lake house?"

"No way," responded Declan. "We probably would run out of gas and be lost in the middle of nowhere."

"Perhaps," spoke Mom. "Now what do you think you will achieve in life if you don't take time, **DREAM**, and develop your roadmap which includes hundreds or thousands of '**X's** along the way?"

"There's no telling," relayed Sophie. "It will probably not be what we wanted to achieve."

"I think you two understand the power of **GOALS** or as we like to say, the '**X' that marks the spot**," said Dad. "**GOALS** are the mini-milestones that you establish on the way to your big, crazy **DREAMS**."

"We're getting very close to the end of our building blocks," responded Mom. "Your Dad and I can tell how far you two have come in just this short time. We're very proud of the both of you."

"Have these lessons helped?" asked Dad.

"They sure have" answered Sophie. "It's like we've been given the secret roadmap to help us navigate the real-life maze course."

"That's exactly right," concluded Dad. "We're so happy that you are seeing it that way."

"Do you **BELIEVE** that you two can achieve any **DREAM** that your heart desires?" inquired Mom.

Both kids replied, "**YES!**"

Mom smiled over at Dad and said, "I don't think they'll have a problem with next week's lesson."

With a big smile on Dad's face, he replied, "**YES** dear, I **BELIEVE** you are right!"

CHAPTER 25

Y is for YES

The following Sunday, Mom and Dad came down the stairs to another incredible breakfast.

"Look Dad, we made your favorite croissant-French toast!" exclaimed Declan.

"Look Mom, we made sure there was extra fruit this morning," added Sophie.

"Wow, this is incredible," remarked Dad. "I know how much your mom loves her fruit, so I'll let her have the fruit and I suppose, I'll just have an extra helping of the croissant-French toast!"

"Funny," laughed Mom. "Kids, put extra fruit on your dad's plate."

"Alright," replied Dad. "Now which kid's turn is it this week at the chalkboard?"

"It's my turn," Sophie said as she approached the chalkboard.

"Have a positive **ATTITUDE!**
BELIEFS lead to achievements!
Make good **CHOICES!**
Chase your **DREAMS!**
EDUCATION does not end at school!

FORGIVENESS to all others!

Always give GRATITUDE!

Give HELP to those in need!

INTEGRITY is doing the right thing, even when no one is looking!

Smile with JOY!

Always show KINDNESS!

LOVE always!

MISTAKES are hidden lessons!

Learn from NATURE!

OBSTACLES are necessary and make the reward sweeter!

PERSISTENCE is never giving up!

NEVER be a QUITTER!

Always accept RESPONSIBILITY!

SEEK and you will find!

We become what we THINK about!

UNIQUENESS is special!

VALOR is strength of mind and spirit!

WORK always comes before the reward!

'X' marks the spot; set goals and define your dreams' mini milestones!

'Y!'...

Does the letter 'Y' stand for YES?" Sophie asked.

"Well done," praised Mom. "It sure does. However, that does not simply mean that you say YES to everything. When we refer to YES, we mean to always have the BELIEF in your abilities. We also mean to have an **ATTITUDE** that tells yourself that **YES**, you can achieve anything."

"No matter how big the **OBSTACLE** is that we face in our maze course, **BELIEVE** that we can get by the **OBSTACLE**. Tell ourselves that **YES** we can!" cheered Declan.

"Precisely," confirmed Dad. "Remember what one of the most successful business owners, Henry Ford said, "Whether you think you can, or you can't, you're RIGHT!""

"Don't fall for the trap of negative thinking. You two now know how important your **THOUGHTS**, **BELIEFS** and **ATTITUDES** are. They help you keep **PERSISTANCE** needed to overcome the **OBSTACLES** that you will undoubtably encounter on your journey toward your **DREAMS**. Not if, but when things get difficult on your journey, always remember… **YES YOU CAN**."

"I like that," smiled Sophie. "**YES, I CAN!**"

"You mean, **YES, WE CAN**," added Declan.

"That's right, **YES, WE CAN!**" Sophie repeated.

"Now you understand why your Dad and I don't allow *I can't* to be said?" questioned Mom.

"You just said I can't," grinned Declan.

"So, did you," Sophie pointed out!

"Okay, okay," interjected Mom. "That's especially important. By simply saying *YES, I CAN*, before you begin something, you are planting the seed of **BELIEF** in your mind. The **BELIEF** will then lead to a positive **ATTITUDE**. This positive **ATTITUDE** will give you the **PERSISTENCE** needed to carry you through the **OBSTACLES** and **MISTAKES** on your journey towards your **DREAMS**."

"It's like each of the building blocks are all connected," commented Sophie.

"Exactly," agreed Dad. "Everything is connected. **CHOOSE** the keys that you have been taught over the past several months and you will always find peace, happiness and success."

"I can't believe that next week is our last week," sighed Declan.

"Remember, **EDUCATION** doesn't end at school and it will not end when we get to Z," promised Mom.

"That's right," nodded Sophie. "Next, we'll look at the 26 traps to watch out for in our **OBSTACLE** maze course to our **DREAMS**."

"Absolutely," assured Dad. "We love the **ZEAL** that you two have towards our Sunday morning breakfast classes."

"Love the seal?" asked Declan. "You mean flippers?"

"Hahaha," laughed Dad. "Not seal, I said **ZEAL**. Don't worry, we have next week for that one. In the meantime, remember **YES, YOU CAN** pass me the syrup!"

CHAPTER 26

Z is for ZEAL

The following Sunday, Mom and Dad came down the stairs to an empty kitchen.

"Where are the kids?" asked Dad.

"They must still be in bed," replied Mom.

"Should we wake them?" questioned Dad.

"No, let them sleep? They were up late last night," answered Mom.

"Well, since today is the letter 'Z', what do you say we celebrate their kitchen table graduation with your world-famous Christmas egg dish and coffee cake?" inquired Dad.

"That's a great idea," responded Mom. "Get the coffee going."

Thirty minutes later, the kitchen was filled with the smell of eggs, sausage, coffee cake and fruit. As if the oven timer were an alarm clock, Sophie and Declan filed down the stairs.

"Good morning kids," greeted Mom. "Did you sleep well last night?"

"I couldn't fall asleep," admitted Sophie. "I knew this was our last morning with our A-to-Z lessons on success," she said sadly.

"Yeah," added Declan. "We're going to miss our Sunday morning breakfast lessons."

"Remember what we taught you," insisted Dad. "Your **EDUCATION** doesn't end at school, and it doesn't end at the breakfast table. Besides, next we're going to review the twenty-six traps that you must watch for and avoid through your real-life **OBSTACLE** maze course to your **DREAMS**."

"That's right!" exclaimed Sophie. "We get more lessons!"

"For completing your first breakfast table education class, we're celebrating your graduation with Christmas eggs and coffee cake!" exclaimed Mom.

"Hooray!" both kids shouted.

"Okay, so who's turn is it at the chalk board?" asked Dad.

"My turn!" exclaimed Declan, as he rushed to the chalk board.

"Have a positive **ATTITUDE!**

BELIEFS lead to achievements!

Make good **CHOICES!**

Chase your **DREAMS!**

EDUCATION does not end at school!

FORGIVENESS to all others!

Always give **GRATITUDE!**

Give **HELP** to those in need!

INTEGRITY is doing the right thing, even when no one is looking!

Smile with **JOY!**

Always show **KINDNESS!**

LOVE always!

MISTAKES are hidden lessons!

Learn from **NATURE!**

OBSTACLES are necessary and make the reward sweeter!

PERSISTENCE is never giving up!

NEVER be a **QUITTER!**

Always accept **RESPONSIBILITY!**

SEEK and you will find!

We become what we **THINK** about!

UNIQUENESS is special!

VALOR is strength of mind and spirit!

WORK always comes before the reward!

'X' marks the spot, set goals and define your dreams' mini milestones!

YES, you can!

'Z!'...

'Z' is for Zebra?" Declan asked, with a puzzled look on his face.

"No," laughed Mom. "However, Zebras sure are pretty animals."

"This is a tough one," said Sophie. "I've learned to pay attention especially through the end of each lesson. I finally figured out that you've been giving us the next week's word at the end of each lesson."

"Wow, impressive!" smiled Dad. "So, what is today's word?"

"'Z' is for **ZEAL**," Sophie replied confidently.

"Excellent!" praised Mom. "Do you know what that means?"

"I have no idea," shrugged Sophie.

"Well, no worries," assured Mom. "You're about to find out."

"**ZEAL** is great energy, or enthusiasm in pursuit of a cause or an objective. Pursuing your **DREAMS** with **ZEAL**, is pursuing them with a passion. Being **ZEALOUS** with your pursuit will further strengthen your **ATTITUDE** and **BELIEF** that you will achieve your **DREAMS**," described Mom.

"Remember, not if, but when you face **OBSTACLES** or make **MISTAKES** on your journey, having a **ZEAL** about your steadfast approach, will help you keep your **PERSISTENCE** and **NEVER** give up," remarked Dad. "Pursuing your **DREAMS** with **ZEAL** will also feed your inner **VALOR** and make the **WORK** seem light. It will indeed give you a **YES**-can spirit."

"Wow!" cheered Sophie. "I figured this would be an important word, but I didn't realize how important it would be."

"That's right," nodded Mom. "The larger the **DREAM**, the larger the **ZEAL** you must possess to capture the **DREAM**."

"So, what do you two think of the lessons we've discussed over the past several months?" questioned Dad.

"Dad, I now understand that it's not luck or circumstance that determines what you achieve. By self-discipline of following these keys you can succeed," explained Sophie.

"Yeah," winked Declan. "I'm ready to chase my **DREAMS** through the **OBSTACLE** maze course of life!"

"That's great," laughed Dad. "Your first **OBSTACLE** on your course is getting through me for the last piece of cake!"

The END... or is it?

ABOUT THE AUTHOR

Brian is a loving husband and father of two amazing children. Like most fathers, Brian wants nothing more than for his children to be instruments of God's love. He also wants to equip them with the tools needed to exceed in the challenging world. Brian believes that the more powerful we can show up in our own lives, the more we can help our community and friends in need.

Brian was passed down the gift of story telling from his father. Cherishing the many stories Brian heard growing up, he wanted to have the same affect on his children and perhaps, one day, their children.

Printed in the United States
by Baker & Taylor Publisher Services